Taking the World,
by Storm

Cover photo courtesy of Gene Tomko

Any information given in this book is solely from the memory of Warren Storm. And although at eighty-two years, Warren's memory is strong–remembering over seventy years of dates, labels, musical venues, friends, bands, and musicians–it is likely that some may have been unintentionally missed or erroneously stated.

ALL PHOTOS ARE COURTESY OF WARREN STORM UNLESS OTHERWISE NOTED

For more information on dancehalls mentioned throughout the book,
please visit: https://louisianadancehalls.com/

ISBN 13 (paper): 978-1-946160-51-5

http://ulpress.org
University of Louisiana at Lafayette Press
P.O. Box 43558
Lafayette, LA 70504-3558

Taking the World, by Storm, A Regional Roots Journey with the Godfather of Swamp Pop,
can be purchased online at www.AcousticSounds.com.

Acoustic Sounds, Inc.
P.O. Box 1905
Salina, KS, 67402-1905
Phone: 1-888-926-2564

Printed on acid-free paper in Canada
Library of Congress Cataloging-in-Publication Data

Names: Storm, Warren, interviewee. | Landry, Yvette, interviewer, compiler.

Title: Taking the world, by storm : a conversation with Warren "Storm"
Schexnider, the godfather of swamp pop / Yvette Landry.
Description: Lafayette : University of Louisiana at Lafayette Press, 2019.
Identifiers: LCCN 2019025428 | ISBN 9781946160515 (hardback)
Subjects: LCSH: Storm, Warren. | Drummers--Louisiana--Biography. |
Musicians--Louisiana--Interviews. | Swamp pop music--Louisiana--History
and criticism.
Classification: LCC ML419.S799 A5 2019 | DDC 781.643092 [B]--dc23
LC record available at https://lccn.loc.gov/2019025428

Taking the World, *by Storm*

A Conversation with

Warren "Storm" Schexnider

The Godfather of Swamp Pop

YVETTE LANDRY

2019
University of Louisiana at Lafayette Press

Warren Storm and Yvette Landry (Photo by Daniel Sanda)

To the memory of my wife, Harriet Schexnider, my family, and all of the swamp pop fans out there—especially Yvette Landry and Luke Bourque.

-Warren Storm

For my husband, Luke, who gave me the vision, space, time, and heart to take on this project.
And for Stan—a true gem.

-Yvette Landry

FOREWORD

—Marc Broussard

Growing up as the son of a legendary sideman in South Louisiana, I was exposed to some of the best singers in the region. Warren Storm was *the* one that loomed large in my young mind. I knew his name long before I ever heard him sing. I understood at an early age that Warren was a legend…and with good reason. His soulful voice, the likes of which I had never heard before, solidified his legendary status for me. And his almost zen-like predisposition to happiness is contagious.

Warren's story has been one of his own making. As is the case for many a career musician, it's never been an easy road to travel, but it is one that allows a man like Warren to carve out his own path and plant his flag in whatever ground he can cover.

I've had the great pleasure of spending time with Warren on a number of occasions. By far, the most memorable was when I joined members of the Lil Band O' Gold on a mission to take Warren to see the movie *Ray*. I had just received my first "mailbox money" for a song I'd written and was excited to share the news. Upon hearing of my new fortunes, Warren congratulated me, then proceeded to ask me for a loan in the exact amount I'd just received…all in jest of course. After the film, Warren proclaimed, "That's the best movie I've seen in decades! But you know, I haven't been to the movies since the 60s!"

The impression from that night with Warren has held firm in my mind. To me, Warren is a man perpetually in search of a good laugh, if not a good time. I doubt he's ever met a stranger, and if this book is any indication, I'm not far off the mark. He's been a road warrior and an icon for Louisiana swamp pop music for over seven decades, and he's showing no signs of slowing down. Vocally, he still sounds as good as ever! As I travel throughout the United States, I see Warren's picture hanging in clubs and venues. It makes me smile every time I see it. Those autographed head shots, commemorating Warren's performances in those rooms, signal to me that I'm no swamp pop pioneer. On the contrary! Louisiana musicians have been paving the way since well before I showed up, yet few have done it with the style and flavor of Warren Storm.

"*Taking the World, by Storm: A Conversation with Warren "Storm" Schexnider* is exactly what I hoped it would be: a conversation with Warren Storm."

Yvette Landry has done an incredible job by just getting out of Warren's way, allowing him to tell us his story. *His* life through *his* eyes, requiring little more than bringing him back on track from time to time, as his stories often lead to places no one saw coming at the start.

One over-arching theme that keeps re-emerging is the awe that Warren has for so many aspects of his charmed existence. "Can you believe it?!" is a phrase he utters with a regularity that suggests he, himself, does NOT believe his own story at times. And indeed, it's easy to see why. I can sympathize, as I myself have often found it hard to believe that a little Cajun boy from South Louisiana could find himself in such incredible situations. From hanging with Elvis at Graceland to hanging backstage with Jerry Lee Lewis or sharing the stage with Robert Plant, Warren Storm has lived a life full of wonder. It's amazing he remembers it all! Thankfully for us, not only does he remember the broad strokes but also the little details, and he's got no issues sharing his perspective as well as his photographs.

I am grateful for the honor of knowing him. Befriending a legend is always a surreal thing, but Warren showed me, more than any other, that titles mean nothing if you can't hang. In all of our interactions, Warren has never asked anything of me beyond my company. And in an industry full of people making judgments about how much you can help their careers, refreshingly, Warren is just looking for some friends to jam with. Luckily for him, there's no shortage of the willing.

So, if you like a good conversation with a good friend, you've found a companion like no other. All you've got to do is prompt Warren, and the stories begin to flow. In this book, Yvette Landry does just that, skillfully, like only a truly great writer can. Prompt Warren and he will take care of the rest. He'll have you smiling and laughing the whole way.

Of special note is Yvette's singular dedication to this project and the mission behind it. As is the case with so many veteran musicians, Warren is no rich man. In fact, he'll probably be singing and working until he physically can't. Yvette has taken it upon herself to try and give Warren some relief, and thus, this project was born. All proceeds from the sale of this book will go to Warren Storm. By buying this book, you are helping a dear friend of mine take a break from the road after 70+ years of dedication to his craft. For that, I cannot thank you enough.

> "In all of nature, no storm can last forever"
>
> —Dr. Wayne Dyer

THE YEAR WAS 1979. The night, sweltering and mosquito filled. The bar, smoky and dim. I recall, as I jitterbugged, two-stepped, and waltzed my way around the worn, wooden, cornmeal sprinkled floor, my love of Louisiana swamp pop music igniting.

Pat's Showboat Club was a cypress-studded, sweatbox bar situated on Bayou Amy in Henderson, Louisiana. It was, and still is (although now Pat's Atchafalaya Club), home to some of Louisiana's most legendary swamp pop bands. All the greats, T.K. Hulin, G.G. Shinn, Joe Douglas, Rod Bernard, Johnnie Allan, Tommy McLain, Cookie and the Cupcakes, and of course, the "Godfather" himself, Warren Storm, had played there. Although many of these musical greats pepper the memories of my youth, none left an impression quite like Warren Storm.

In my mind, even at the young age of only seventeen, Warren was a legend. He remains one today. And although he was very approachable and lived only twenty miles away, as the crow flies, it wasn't until 2017 that I actually had the opportunity to not only meet him, but also shake his hand.

I knew very little about the man; only that I loved his voice, almost as much as I loved his mustache. And that laugh! Who wouldn't fall in love with that laugh? Add to the fact that he could play drums (my grandfather, brother, and son's instrument), well…it goes without saying that getting to meet "The Godfather of Louisiana Swamp Pop" was on my bucket list for sure.

****

Warren Schexnider was born February 18, 1937, in the small town of Leroy, an area located between Maurice and Abbeville, Louisiana. He and his family lived with his grandparents in an Acadian-style home while Warren attended school from first through third grades. After the birth of his sister, Verna Schexnider, the family moved to Abbeville. His mother, Lois Meaux, was a homemaker. His father, Simon Schexnailder, spent his days working as a sharecropper and his nights working as a musician, neither of which brought in a suitable income. According to Warren…

> "I was born poor, and I'm still poor."

What follows is a series of interviews and conversations with Warren at his home and various places in and around Broussard, Louisiana.

YL: Warren, tell me about these photos.

WS: That was me when I was just a couple of years old. That's from the beginning. You know what they used to tell me? We had the sewing machine with the knobs on it and I'd make as if that was a radio. And the flyswatter, I'd make as if that was a guitar.

WS: That's me and Mama. I think I kind of look like her. They called her *"Lo-ez"* in French.

WS: That's my daddy [*far right*]. He must have been two or three years old. They told me he didn't want to take a picture so he did like that with his shoulder. They wanted to hold him but they put him on a chair instead.

WS: Look at them shoes, man! Oh, my goodness.

WS: That's my dad. That was probably way before I was born. I'm guessing this was probably at the beginning of the 1930s.

YL: He's a handsome man.

WS: Yep. He's much more handsome than me. [*laughing*] That's my dad again, Simon. He had blue eyes. Mine are brown. I wish I'd have had his blue eyes.

Top: Warren Schexnider (1940)

Far left: Warren and his mother, Lois Meaux Schexnailder

Left: Lois Meaux Schexnailder (Warren's mother)

Simon Schexnailder (Warren's father)

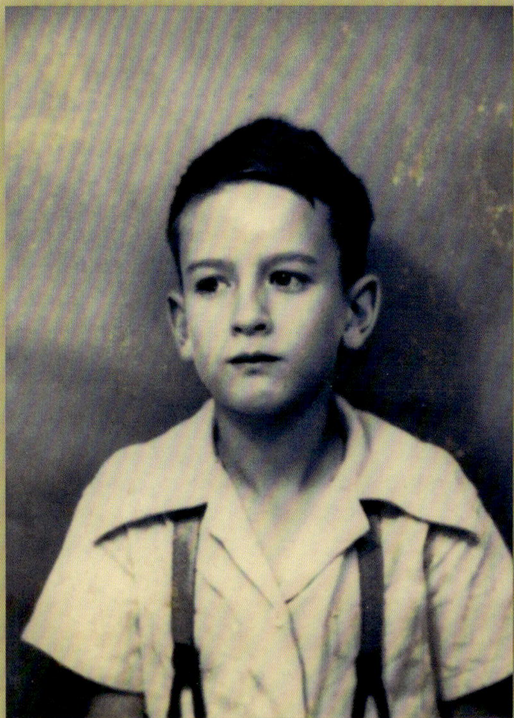

School Days

WS: Lord have mercy. I guess I was about seven years old.

YL: Was that a school picture?

WS: No. That was just a family picture. Look at those suspenders!

WS: Now that's a school picture. I started wearing glasses when I was twelve. I was born in 1937 so you can figure out how old I was in this picture. Maybe somewhere around fourteen.

WS: [*laughing*] In that first school picture I was eleven years old.

"I spent my time watching my dad play the drums, listening to the *Opry*, and playing my dad's drums."

YL: What was it like growing up?

WS: Times were hard. Life was hard. My daddy drank a lot. We were not that close. He didn't ever say, "I love you." We were more like friends. Mama did, but not that often.

[*Still, as Warren reminisces, looking at pictures, one can see only pleasant memories from his childhood.*]

WS: After working in the fields all day, my daddy would turn to music. He played music all of his life, just like I'm doing. There was a brief stint where he worked for the State of Louisiana Highway Department, but music was his love. He had a band called The Rayne-Bo Ramblers. I think they started, probably around 1937 or the early 1940s, right after I was born. Drums were his instrument of choice, but he played a little fiddle, guitar, and accordion, just to mess around.

Verna Schexnider and Warren Storm (Red Barn, Abbeville, LA, 2012)

WS: My daddy died of a stomach aneurysm at the age of sixty-six. He played drums until he was about sixty years old. My mom had a stroke four years before she died. She passed at the age of eighty-one years old.

YL: Do you have your father's drums or any of his instruments?

WS: I don't have any of his drums. But I've got one of mine in the Swamp Pop Hall of Fame in Ville Platte, Louisiana; you gotta visit that sometime. I don't have his accordion or fiddle either. I had seen the accordion, but it was so old that it was all demolished. My sister kept the fiddle and I don't know what happened to it. I got one sister. She lives in Abbeville–Verna Schexnider. She's eleven years younger than I am.

WS: You gotta remember, times were tough back then. When we moved to Abbeville, we didn't even have electricity. We had oil lamps, and a battery radio. I used to listen to the *Grand Ole Opry* on that battery radio. That's when I first heard of Hank Snow, Hank Williams Sr., and Faron Young. Faron was from Louisiana. The show played on Saturdays. I was eleven, or something like that, and I spent my time watching my dad play the drums, listening to the Opry, and playing my dad's drums.

Verna Schexnider (Warren's sister, 1953)

YL: Where did Simon play?

WS: Dad played in some little honky-tonk in Abbeville. I don't even remember the name of the place. It was just an old honky-tonk.

YL: Did you have a favorite singer that you couldn't wait to hear on the *Grand Old Opry*?

WS: [*without hesitation*] Hank Williams Sr. That's the one. He had so much soul in his voice, just like George Jones did, that was another favorite of mine. Some kinda way, he had "country soul." Just like Elvis, they were influenced by old blues men from around Montgomery, Alabama, and Mississippi. They went listen to those old blues men while they were young, before they found their voice. So, they got some soul out of that. And so did I!

YL: Who else influenced you vocally besides Hank Williams Sr. and George Jones?

WS: Well, Ray Price was one of the greatest singers of all times. But all the old country singers was my favorites. And Fats Domino, but I'll talk about him later.

YL: Did your mother play music?

WS: No. My mom wasn't a musician. She didn't really even listen to the radio program. It was me and my daddy that listened to it. Basically, it was just me though. I can remember Hank Williams. That voice! Can you imagine what I felt like when I actually met Hank Williams Sr. in 1948? He was on the *Hadacol Caravan*, and I watched him get down from the stage and I shook his hand. Man, I wish I had a camera at that time, but I was eleven years old. I was such a huge fan. He came down the steps from the stage in his white suit. I'm sure you remember the famous white suit and hat. And I was right by the speakers on the side of the stage. I stood there and listened to him sing "Hey Good Looking." I thought that was so amazing. When he was done, he didn't talk to me, but he shook my hand. Later, I met his son, Hank Williams Jr., and his grandson, Hank Williams III. Luckily, I had a camera with me at that time. I've got pictures with them, but Hank...man...

YL: Where was this picture taken?

WS: That was in Kinder, Louisiana, in 2011. I had met him years before when he had just started playing at the old Pangay's Club, but I had never taken a picture with him. I got to go on his bus too! I had friends that knew him well. He used to go fishing with them down in Grand Chenier; they were good buddies. But, he doesn't do that anymore since all of the shootings have happened. Now he goes straight from the bus to the stage. You can't even go on his bus anymore. I was just fortunate to do that! And we talked a long while. I told him, "I've been playing music all my life." He said, "Me too!" He was very nice. He had some of his family with him, his daughters. He wasn't drinking or doing drugs at the time. He was really nice.

YL: Tell me about how you were able to meet Hank Williams III.

WS: Well, that was right here in Lafayette at Grant Street Dancehall. A friend of mine was playing bass with Hank III, and invited us to the show, backstage, and then onto the bus afterwards.

YL: Did you tell him that you met both his father and grandfather?

WS: Yes, I did. He was thrilled about that.

WS: You know, he did his grandfather's songs in the first half of his set. Then the next part, he took his hair down and did some rock-n-roll. [*pauses*] That was weird, man! He was weird, but I'm glad I got to meet all three of them.

YL: Let's get back to your younger days.

Top: Hank Williams Jr. and Warren Storm (2011)

Bottom left: Warren Storm and Hank Williams Jr. (Hank's bus, Kinder, LA, 2010)

Bottom right: Warren Storm and Hank Williams III (Grant Street Dancehall, Lafayette, LA)

WS: After we moved from Leroy, I went to school in Abbeville. I graduated from Abbeville High at the age of nineteen, in 1956. We lived right in back of the old school. It was there that I met my friend, and fellow Abbevillian, Bobby Charles. He was in grades with me. Later, he went across the river and went to the Catholic school. Eventually we reconnected and played music together.

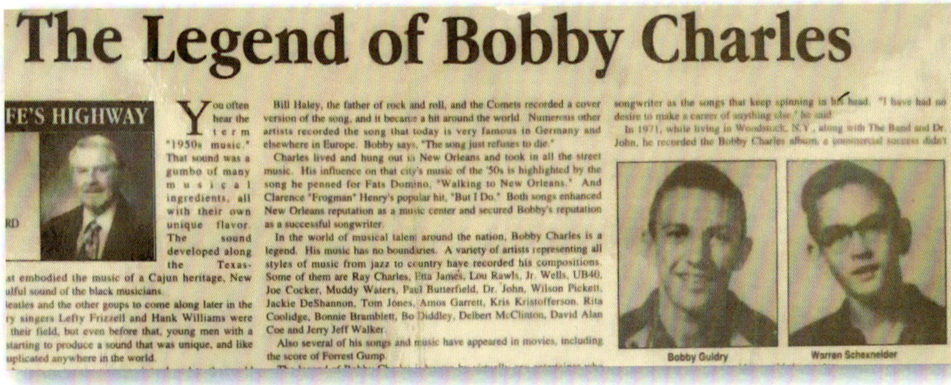

The Legend of Bobby Charles

FE'S HIGHWAY

RD

You often hear the term "1950s music." That sound was a gumbo of many musical ingredients, all with their own unique flavor. The sound developed along the Texas-

...at embodied the music of a Cajun heritage, New ...ulful sound of the black musicians.

...eatles and the other goups to come along later in the ...ry singers Lefty Frizzell and Hank Williams were ... their field, but even before that, young men with a ...starting to produce a sound that was unique, and like ...uplicated anywhere in the world.

Bill Haley, the father of rock and roll, and the Comets recorded a cover version of the song, and it became a hit around the world. Numerous other artists recorded the song that today is very famous in Germany and elsewhere in Europe. Bobby says, "The song just refuses to die."

Charles lived and hung out in New Orleans and took in all the street music. His influence on that city's music of the '50s is highlighted by the song he penned for Fats Domino, "Walking to New Orleans." And Clarence "Frogman" Henry's popular hit, "But I Do." Both songs enhanced New Orleans reputation as a music center and secured Bobby's reputation as a successful songwriter.

In the world of musical talent around the nation, Bobby Charles is a legend. His music has no boundaries. A variety of artists representing all styles of music from jazz to country have recorded his compositions. Some of them are Ray Charles, Etta James, Lou Rawls, Jr. Wells, UB40, Joe Cocker, Muddy Waters, Paul Butterfield, Dr. John, Wilson Pickett, Jackie DeShannon, Tom Jones, Amos Garrett, Kris Kristofferson, Rita Coolidge, Bonnie Bramblett, Bo Diddley, Delbert McClinton, David Alan Coe and Jerry Jeff Walker.

Also several of his songs and music have appeared in movies, including the score of Forrest Gump.

songwriter as the songs that keep spinning in his head. "I have had no desire to make a career of anything else," he said.

In 1971, while living in Woodstock, N.Y., along with The Band and Dr. John, he recorded the Bobby Charles album, a commercial success didn't

Bobby Guidry

Warren Schexneider

WS: It's a funny story how Bobby and me got started. He'd come to my house and pick me up. He had a car and I didn't. But I had the tape recorder though, and a guitar! So, we'd go to his sister's house and record some tunes that he wrote so he could send them to New Orleans.

WS: Roy Dunn wrote up an article about Bobby. I've got it somewhere. It's an interesting story.

YL: Tell me about this picture of you, Bobby, and Johnnie.

WS: Bobby Charles used to live in Milton; he had a place on the Vermilion River. Me and Johnnie Allan went see him one afternoon in 1988. We just visited and talked about music and everything.

YL: Bobby Charles had a bar?

WS: No! It was his little shack on the river. He had all kinds of stuff in there. He was kind of a weird dude towards the end.

YL: I know you went to school together and played music when you were younger, but were you ever in a band together?

WS: Oh yeah! I played drums in his band. We played all over Louisiana. And I recorded with him. I was actually driving the car when he wrote "Walking to New Orleans!" He was sitting in the backseat and I was driving. We were childhood friends and friends until the end.

WS: What's the best moment, or most unique moment, you had with Bobby Charles?

WS: Well, we had a unique moment. Remember, I had a tape recorder and he didn't. And I played a little bit guitar, and he didn't. So, when we'd get together, I'd play the chords and he'd write the song in his head. He'd just sing it to me. See, he wasn't a musician. But when he wrote the song, he had the melody with it. So that's genius right there!

YL: He would just sing the melody?

WS: Yes. And whenever he went in the studio, the musicians would just figure out the chords and everything.

Warren Storm, Bobby Charles, and Johnnie Allan (Maurice, LA, 1988)

YL: Had you learned more than three chords on the guitar yet?

WS: Well, three or four maybe…five on a good day.

YL: Bobby Charles was known for his song writing skills. Did you ever write songs?

WS: Nope. I just sang them.

WS: Did you know Bobby Charles once sat at the table with Willie Nelson?

YL: No, I didn't. Did you ever meet Willie Nelson?

WS: Me? Of course I did! I got pictures too.

YL: How did you meet Willie Nelson?

WS: I met Willie Nelson's son at the Blue Moon Saloon in Lafayette, Louisiana. He had a gig there. After the gig, I jammed with him and his bass player; I had brought my snare drum. He told me that his dad was on tour and would be playing in Baton Rouge the next day. He said, "If you come, I'll get you in." So, I went. I got to go on Willie's bus and backstage! I told Willie, "I jammed with your son last night." That's how I got to meet Willie Nelson.

YL: Did you go by yourself?

WS: No. My son came with me.

YL: Did you just go in and out of the bus, or did you get a chance to sit and visit with Willie Nelson?

WS: Yes, we visited! We took pictures on his bus with him and his sister. She plays piano with him.

YL: Did he know who you were?

WS: Yes. He had heard of me through Bobby Charles.

WS: At first, he didn't. But I knew he knew who Bobby Charles was. I told him that I was good friends with Bobby Charles and then he said, "Oh yeah! I know who you are!"

Top: Warren Storm and Willie Nelson (Texas Club, Baton Rouge, LA, 2013)

Bottom: Warren Storm, Todd Schexnider, Bobbie Nelson, and Willie Nelson (Baton Rouge, LA, 2013)

YL: Most people would say that you and Bobby Charles are pretty famous. Do you think that's true?

WS: We got our signs up in Abbeville! Coming in from Erath, by the airport, it says, "Welcome to Historic Abbeville, Home of Warren Storm, Swamp Pop Pioneer."

WS: I'm like Daniel Boone! A pioneer! [*pauses*]

WS: Well, I'm more like a Godfather! [*laughing*]

YL: Exactly how did you become the "Godfather of Swamp Pop"?

WS: In the early 90s, I played a swamp pop concert in Gonzales, Louisiana. A friend of mine, Ronnie Richey, he passed away years ago, made a comment that I was the oldest performer playing swamp pop. He said, "Well...I guess you the Godfather!" I said, "I guess so." And the name just stuck with me.

WS: Ronnie wasn't even a musician. He was just a good friend who loved music, but the name stuck. I'm older than all of them—Van Broussard, Johnnie Allan, Tommy McLain—yep, I'm the Godfather!

Warren Storm (Abbeville High School Band, 1956)

Warren Storm (High School Graduation, 1956)

YL: Let's go back to Abbeville High School. Did you play music there?

WS: I had been playing drums and a little guitar in my dad's band, but never in school. Then, my senior year, the band director asked me to play drums. I told him that I didn't read music, but if he'd play it through once, I'd get the beat. He said, "OK." That's how much he believed in me.

WS: But I'd been playing the drums for almost nine years by that time.

YL: Tell me about this picture in the band uniform. Where was this taken?

WS: That was taken at a parade in Abbeville during the Dairy Festival. Now it's called the Cattle Festival.

Lucky Go Ramblers

The Rayne-Bo Ramblers (1941)

YL: So, your father was a musician.

WS: Yes. He had a band called The Rayne-Bo Ramblers. I think they started probably around 1937 or early 1940s, right after I was born. He had the Lucky Go Ramblers too.

WS: The Lucky Go Ramblers of Abbeville. Look at that, they had guitar and no bass; just fiddle, guitar, mandolin, and drums.

YL: What kind of music did they play?

WS: Probably hillbilly-country music.

YL: Do you think they played bluegrass, or old-time music?

WS: I don't know. I have no clue on that. But they did have a radio program on KVOL–a long time ago.

YL: Your dad played on that program?

WS: Probably so. With some of them bands that he started. I remember seeing one band. I must have been seven or eight years old when I went to see them.

YL: What was it like to go to watch your dad play at eight years old?

Simon Schexnailder (1945)

WS: When my daddy would take me to the dances with him, he was playing those little honky-tonks in Abbeville or Landry's Palladium in Lafayette. He played with different musicians like J.B. Perry. I'd go sit on the bandstand and sometimes I'd fall asleep.

YL: What was your first gig?

WS: I was eleven, and daddy was sick one night. I took his place.

YL: Had you played before?

WS: Well, just at home.

YL: So it was his band, The Rayne-Bo Ramblers, that you played with the first time?

WS: Yes.

YL: Did your dad drive you to the gig?

WS: Well no, the band picked me up.

YL: Were you nervous?

WS: [*laughing*] I can't remember if I was nervous…I wanted to play so bad, you know.

YL: I know this is a stretch, but do you remember the first song you played with the band?

WS: No. I just remember it was called hillbilly music back then, but it was really country music. You know we played all the standards back then, probably a lot of Hank Sr.'s songs, like "Move It On Over" and all, you know [*pause*] "Cold, Cold, Heart…." [*chuckles*]

YL: Now at the time, you were only playing the drums, correct?

WS: I was eleven, yes.

YL: Ok, so you played that one gig…

WS: Then some other musicians, other band members from around the area, they had a little band, different bands, so I played with them, mostly on Saturday nights.

WS: The first paycheck I got, on a Saturday night, was $4.50.

YL: Really?! You remember that?

WS: [*laughing*] Yeah.

YL: How long was the gig?

WS: Aw, it was probably four hours…with a break, you know.

WS: But I had a big 28-inch bass drum. You could barely see me behind the drum 'cause I was a small kid.

YL: Whose drums were you using?

WS: My dad's.

YL: So, if you played a gig, your dad couldn't play, correct?

WS: Right.

YL: He'd give up his gigs so you could play?

WS: Yeah. I eventually got a set, when I was about seventeen.

YL: How'd you get the money to buy a set?

WS: Well, I was making $4.50 every Saturday.

YL: So basically, when you started playing music, your dad's career was done?

WS: Well, it wasn't *done*…he'd play once in a while. Remember, he was a sharecropper, you know. He'd have to take care of that work.

A short version of my memories surrounding the colorful life of everyone's friend, Mr. Warren "Storm" Schexnider.

I first met Warren when he was fifteen years old while he was the drummer in the late Larry Brasseaux Band. Other musicians were Nelson "Nap" Lange (fiddle), "Bibb" Stelly (steel guitar)...don't remember the others, so, "just ask Warren." Mr. Roy Theriot was mayor of Abbeville at the time and became Louisiana State Comptroller for many years. Mr. Theriot was always a great promoter of local artists. This function was a benefit held at a school gymnasium. The highlight part of the program was when the mayor introduced this fifteen-year-old drummer and thanked him for participating in the benefit program.

Warren was always the smiling face at all gatherings. He was a great asset to the city of Lafayette as a worker in their printing shop. His boss was the late Leroy Castille, one of the original swamp pop saxophonists. I was honored to work with Mr. Carroll Rachou, owner of La Louisianne Records and Recording Studio. Warren was always there, always with his WS perpetual smile. Others in the group were Glenn Himel (piano), George "Muscles" Belote (bass), and Jack LeBlanc (guitar). Always with us, giving helping hands and scheduling, was Mr. Rachou's longtime assistant, Eddy Raven.

Three of the times I saw Warren the happiest ever was when Harold Romero booked him to play drums and sing with Nashville's famous Buddy Emmons (pedal steel guitar) and Phil Baugh (lead guitarist). This was a Saturday evening at old Pangay's near Cade in the spring of 1982. The next time I saw him the happiest was two-fold. First, I picked him up to drive him to Buck and Johnny's in Breaux Bridge to see and meet Yvette Landry. He had been hearing about her for years. Also playing that night was a mutual friend, Richard "T-Coe" Comeaux, who played music for a long time with the group Little Band O' Gold. They were roommates on the road and I knew Richard would have tons of good stories. I recently found an old cassette with the recording of the entire Emmons/Baugh concert. I soon converted it to CDs, one especially for Warren. Leaving Warren's place, I played the CD; Warren went wild. He took the volume control and became the happiest man on earth.

"Warren was always the smiling face at all gatherings."

As mentioned above, this day was a two-fold happy day. Arriving at Buck and Johnny's, Warren was greeted as royalty, love at first sight. Before the show, Yvette asked me if I thought it would be OK if she sang one of Warren's song, "I Need Somebody Bad Tonight." She sang it, Warren went wild again, and quickly said, "This is the first time I hear a girl sing that song." In my humble opinion, this bond between Yvette and Warren will never be broken.

There are a couple of X-rated stories about Warren as a teenager. All I can say is, ask Warren about the advice given to him by band leader and drummer, Luby Landry of Kaplan. Also, ask Warren about the advice and assistance given to him by Pressley Maturin of Maurice.

My congratulations to Yvette for the future book, on the life of Warren Storm.

—Milton Guilbeau

YL: And the band would come pick you up?

WS: Yes. Different local bands around there. Then, when I was seventeen, I started playing with Larry Brasseaux. I had my own set, and daddy continued playing with different groups…Happy Fats, and bands like that.

YL: Where did you get your set of drums?

WS: From Romero's Music Company in New Iberia, Louisiana.

WS: And, plus, I got another set from Prof Erny's in Lafayette too. So I had two sets of drums.

YL: You must have been making money if you had two sets of drums?

WS: Yeah. I was playing with Larry Brasseaux. His band was called Larry Brasseaux and The Rhythmairs. We were playing like three, four gigs every week.

WS: We were just four pieces. Larry played rhythm guitar, I played drums, Nelson Lange played the fiddle, and Jeffery Stelly played the steel guitar. Dalton Delcambre took Jeffery Stelly's place. We played mostly hillbilly and popular music.

YL: Explain popular music.

WS: Beats me. All was invited. The public would come. People would put the posters up at different stores and filling stations. They put them on telephone poles too… mostly telephone poles. Anywhere you could stick them, they'd put a poster to get the word out.

YL: How old were you at this point?

WS: Sixteen or seventeen, somewhere around there. I wasn't even Warren Storm yet.

YL: Had you graduated high school at this point?

Larry Brasseaux and the Rhythmairs (1954)

WS: Not yet. I didn't graduate until I was nineteen. I had flunked one year.

YL: What grade did you fail?

WS: Third grade, I believe. [*laughing*]

YL: Did you misbehave in school?

WS: [*still laughing*] I don't know. When I went to school, I couldn't speak English. French was my first language.

YL: Did you work in the field as well?

WS: Yes, I picked cotton and red pepper, I mean cayenne pepper, and I picked sweet potatoes...out of the ground.

YL: Were your bandmates from the Abbeville area?

WS: Larry Brasseaux was from Henry, about ten miles south of Abbeville, and the others were from Erath and Abbeville.

YL: Who had the vehicle?

The Seranaiders (1957)

The Rainbow Inn (Kaplan, 1958)

WS: Larry did. He had a pickup truck with a cab. Sometimes I'd have to ride in the back with the instruments though! [*laughs*]

YL: How long did you play with Larry Brasseaux and the Rhythmairs?

WS: I played three years with Larry. Then, after that, I played with another band from New Iberia, Herb Landry's band called The Seranaiders.

WS: The Seranaiders–Otis Tauzin, Warren Storm, Herb Landry, and Pressley Maturin, from Maurice.

YL: At that time, were you still just playing hillbilly music?

WS: Naw, when I went with Herb, I stopped. When Fats Domino came out, and I heard him, I said, "I wanna learn that kinda music!" So, Herb played the sax, and this was like old rhythm and blues we were playing then.

YL: What year was that?

WS: This was in 1957, after I graduated. I think I was twenty years old.

YL: Were you only playing in the Abbeville area?

WS: No, we played like Morgan City, Franklin, Jeanerette, Abbeville...back then they had umpteen clubs. Every little community had a club. When I played with Herb Landry, we were the first band to open up La Louisiane, in New Iberia. Then we played at the Casa Blanca and the Oriental Club. Both of those were in New Iberia too.

YL: Anywhere else?

WS: Kaplan. And they had Prims, around Delcambre out there. Then going to Abbeville from Lafayette, they had at the curve there, they had Palombo's Night Club...we played there too.

YL: What about Breaux Bridge, or St. Martinville, or anywhere in St. Martin Parish?

WS: I played in Breaux Bridge. St. Martinsville, at Signoreli's. I played at the four corners in Cecilia at Shookta's and Pat's in Henderson, this side of the river. I played there with Herb Landry when I was seventeen.

The Wee Wow's (Martinez's Dance Hall, Morse, LA, 1955)

YL: So, it was Pat's first, then it became Pat's Showboat Club, and now it's Pat's Atchafalaya...

WS: Yes, now you have to cross the river to get to Pat's, but before that it was on this side of the river.

YL: We're back in 1957, and you're playing the drums.

WS: Yes. I played three years with Herb Landry and three years with Larry. So, I started with Larry in, let's see, '53, '54, '55. Then '55, '56, '57 with Herb Landry.

YL: At this point were you playing guitar yet?

WS: No. Right after I left Herb Landry I formed my own band called The Wee Wow's. I played drums a little with them, but mostly I played guitar.

WS: Warren Storm and The Wee Wow's. That's me and Ronnie Mayard on sax.

YL: When I look at your old pictures, names and dates are always written on the back. It's curious to me that Schexnider is spelled differently on several pictures. Why is that?

WS: They had six different ways of spelling it. I never spelled my name like my daddy, *Schexnailder*, with an "L"...I went straight to Schexnider.

YL: When you started The Wee Wow's, were you still Warren Schexnider at this point? Or had you become Warren Storm?

WS: I was Warren Storm.

YL: How did that come about?

WS: When I was in high school, they had this famous girl singer. She was an actress too. Her name was Gail Storm, so I got "Storm" from her name.

YL: Why did you want to change your name?

WS: Because Schexnider was too big to put on a 45 record!

YL: I like the microphone in that picture of The Wee Wow's.

WS: How you like that?! I used to have a bunch of them. I don't have them anymore. I wish I did–they're worth a lot of money now! [*laughing*]

YL: Are you self-taught on all instruments?

WS: Yes. Guitar, well, I'd go around the neighborhood. They had three or four guys playing guitar, so I'd go and watch them...learn a few chords...so that's how I learned how to play that.

YL: Where did you get a guitar?

WS: My first guitar was a Stella guitar, I think from Montgomery Wards or one of them stores there.

YL: Did you order it from a magazine?

WS: No. I went pick it up.

YL: That's your first guitar...does that mean you had a second?

WS: Yeah, I had a Kay. The one that I have a picture with in The Wee Wow's. Maybe it was a Sherwood...

YL: Do you still have any guitars?

WS: I got one guitar. I got a Gibson now. I gotta show you that. I been having it about twenty-something years.

YL: Where did you get your Gibson?

WS: That was a friend of mine and his wife who gave me that guitar. Talk about some characters, man. They used to fight all the time. They had a pool hall in Creole, Louisiana. You see that dent right there? That comes from a fight they had. I'm glad it survived. His wife took a pool stick and just started swinging.

WS: Later, when my friend died, his wife gave me the guitar. They would fight like dogs. She'd beat the s*** out of him with a pool stick, man. And, he was a big dude. She was a pretty large woman too, though. They were crazy. They'd get drunk and…[*laughing*] Lord have mercy!

YL: What happened to your Kay?

WS: Oh, I don't know what happened to that thing. [*laughing*] It disintegrated I guess!

WS: And I got three snare drums and three cymbals, no bass drum. I don't have a set anymore.

WS: One of my drums is special. It was made by James Trussart. He wanted me to use it when I played with Lil' Band O' Gold. Look at it…it's golden!

YL: How did you come up with the name Wee Wow's?

WS: Well, everybody was saying, "wow wee," but I changed it and I turned it around and said, "wee wow." That's how I got the name.

WS: We played on Tuesday nights, by Gueydan…what's that place, in Morse, Louisiana…at Martinez's Dance Hall.

YL: Who were the members of The Wee Wow's?

WS: Well, I played the guitar. Ronnie Mayard, he graduated with me, played sax and Lubby Landry (he had his own band too), played the drums, and Dalton Colomb played another guitar and bass. We were just three or four of us. We were just musicians hanging around in the 1950s who happened to get together in some miracle way.

YL: In your first band, you played guitar. Did you sing as well?

WS: Aw yes! I did *all* the singing.

YL: Why did you decide to play guitar instead of drums?

WS: I don't know. I had another band that was just a sideline thing, you know. We'd only play like twice a week–Tuesdays and Sundays–and I'd play drums. Then, I'd play guitar for The Wee Wow gigs on Friday and Saturday.

YL: What was this sideline band called?

WS: The Wanderers.

YL: Do you have a picture of The Wanderers?

WS: No. I wish I did.

YL: Who were the members of that band?

WS: Lafayette musicians.

YL: The Wee Wow's played on Friday and Saturday nights?

WS: Yes. On Saturdays I'd borrow an electric guitar from my dad's friend Woody Guidry. Lubby Landry played drums and Ronnie Mayard played sax. We were just three of us. We didn't have a bass. Before the movies, on the stage at Frank's Theatre in Abbeville, we'd play. I did that for about a year. We'd play for an hour. I ran my guitar through the movie speakers. It was real loud. The kids enjoyed it! They didn't dance. They just sat down like it was a concert, and they had our name on the screen–*Warren Storm and The Wee Wow's*. That was a big thing!

YL: Did they pay you?

WS: Nope. Playing for free! [*laughing*]

YL: What happened to The Wee Wow's?

WS: Everybody went their separate ways.

YL: What band is in these pictures?

WS: Let's see...what did I call myself back then? I had so many damn names. I believe it was called just The Warren Storm Band.

WS: Can you believe Rufus Thibodeaux was on bass? You see, the fiddle wasn't too popular back then in 1960.

YL: Where were these photos taken?

WS: They were taken at Lou Anne's Club on the Louisiana/Texas state line. We'd go there and play for seven weeks.

YL: Why for seven weeks?

The Warren Storm Band (1960) with Al Foreman, guitar; Warren Storm, drums; Murphy Bufford, sax; and Rufus Thibodeaux, bass

YL: What was the name of this band in this Forrest Club picture?

WS: Now what was the name of that band, Warren Storm... I think this was called The Jive Masters.

YL: Where did that come from?

WS: [*laughing*] I don't know. Can you imagine that? The Forrest Club on the Breaux Bridge Highway. They had a lot of clubs there: the Boundary Club, the Forrest Club, and then they had the Midway Club, which later turned into Boo-Boo's Nightclub.

WS: Because down here, during Lent, nobody went to the dances. So we'd go where they didn't observe Lent. We'd play for seven weeks over there, once a year, and that was it. My wife would drive us, and we'd get a room at a roach motel down the road for a week at a time, then we'd drive back to Lafayette. We'd play on Fridays and Saturdays and come back on Sundays. Then we'd go back the next week.

YL: Would they charge people to get into the dance?

WS: Yes, they'd charge a couple of dollars. I was making just $100 a week for the two jobs, but you could buy a bread for 10¢ in 1960, and the gas was like 35¢ a gallon. $100 a week…that's $400 a month.

The Jive Masters (Forrest Club, Breaux Bridge, LA, 1958)

Warren Storm Band (Grand Opening–Frostop, New Iberia, 1958)

YL: Tell me about this picture in 1958.

WS: That's Buster Shilling on sax, Murton Thibodeaux on piano, Al Foreman on guitar, and me, Warren Storm on drums and vocals.

WS: People still talk about that Frostop gig. They must have had about 2,000–3,000 people there. We played on a flatbed truck in the parking lot. People danced and everything.

WS: That's when my "Prisoner's Song" was out. The guy that owned The Frostop, Stan, owned about three or four hundred jukeboxes, and he put my "Prisoner's Song" on all of them!

WS: Can you imagine? I was twenty-one years old! Mercy… Lord have mercy!

YL: Who would run sound?

WS: We'd run our own sound system. I had two very small baffles on each side of the bandstand. We didn't even have monitors. That's it.

YL: I can understand traveling with all of the instruments, but what about the piano player? Did you have to lug a piano around to all of your gigs?

WS: [*laughing*] No. Everywhere we played, they had old pianos. Murton would bring his tuning fork to tune the pianos before the gigs because they were so ancient. Then, we'd just drop a mic inside. It was primitive!

YL: What brand of drums did you play?

WS: Slingerland drums. Gene Krupa advertised for those drums, and he was my first drum idol.

[*Warren pauses…thinking…searching the recesses of his brain…*]

WS: You see, I had two bands at one time. Both bands started in '57–'58. Because we'd play different times. Now in '58, that's when I went to Crowley to record.

YL: How did that come about?

WS: That came about with a guitar player from Abbeville, called Woody Guidry. He knew J.D. Miller. Woody Guidry was a famous guitar player. At that time, he played with Jimmy Davis and everybody.

WS: I was playing at a club in Kaplan called The Rainbow Inn. And Mr. Clifford LeMaire was the owner there. Woody heard me and set the meeting up with J.D. Miller. Clifford LeMaire came to Abbeville and picked me up and brought me to Crowley to audition.

YL: What was Woody doing there?

WS: Well, him and my daddy played music together. I guess he came to watch us.

YL: Just to clarify, Woody was the one who felt you should record?

WS: Yeah. He told J.D. Miller, "You need to listen to this boy from Abbeville."

YL: What was the name of the studio in Crowley?

WS: That was one of the first ones J.D. Miller had. It was on Main Street there, but it's no longer there. They got a bank there now.

YL: Do you remember what it was called?

WS: J. Miller Studio. He was recording Doc Guidry at that time, and Jimmy C. Newman, and Guitar Gable. So, I was like the new kid on the block there when I went and auditioned.

YL: Had J.D. Miller ever heard you sing?

Warren Storm (Recording Session at J.D. Miller, 1959)
(Courtesy of Johnnie Allan, Center for Louisiana Studies, and Special Collections at the University of Louisiana at Lafayette)

WS: No.

YL: What did you sing for your audition?

WS: I sang one of Fats Domino songs, "Blue Monday," I think, one of them songs. J.D. was kind of impressed. So, in a couple of more weeks, I went back and J.D. wrote "Mama, Mama, Mama" for me. J.D. was a great songwriter. And, he also rewrote some words for the "Prisoner's Song," which was already forty years old in '58. It was an old standard, and that became my first recording.

YL: That means you had "Mama, Mama, Mama" on one side and the "Prisoner's Song" on the other?

WS: Yes. I had a double-sided hit on NASCO Records, out of Nashville, TN.

YL: You recorded this record in Crowley. How did NASCO get it?

WS: Well, J.D. was doing business with Ernie Young, from Nashville. He had Excello Records, that was the blues artist label. And the white artist label was NASCO. The Crescendos were on NASCO too when they signed me up with them.

YL: Let's get back to the session where you recorded your first record.

WS: Well, on that session, I played drums on "Mama, Mama, Mama" while singing. And Guitar Gable's drummer played on "Prisoner's Song." His name was Clarence "Jockey" Etienne. Guitar Gable played that guitar run…*da-da-don-da dun*… [*Warren sings the run*…] Both Guitar Gable and Jockey played on the "Prisoner's Song." This was in 1958 and I was twenty-one.

YL: Did the song chart?

WS: Yes, it charted on *Billboard Magazine,* No. 81. It stayed two weeks in the top 100. My first record charted. Man, can you believe that?! [*laughs*]

YL: I've heard stories that artist didn't receive royalties for their records. Was that the case? Did you sign a contract?

WS: I signed a five-year contract with J.D. Miller. I got royalties on the "Prisoner's Song," but only $1,000 in royalties. It sold 250,000 copies. Nowadays, selling 250,000 would be like selling one million copies, so…

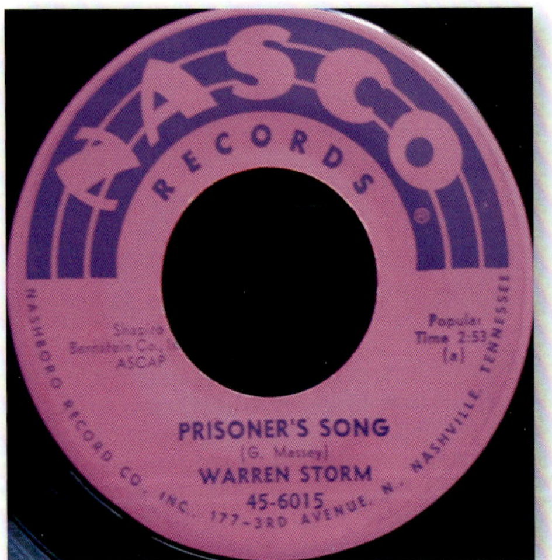

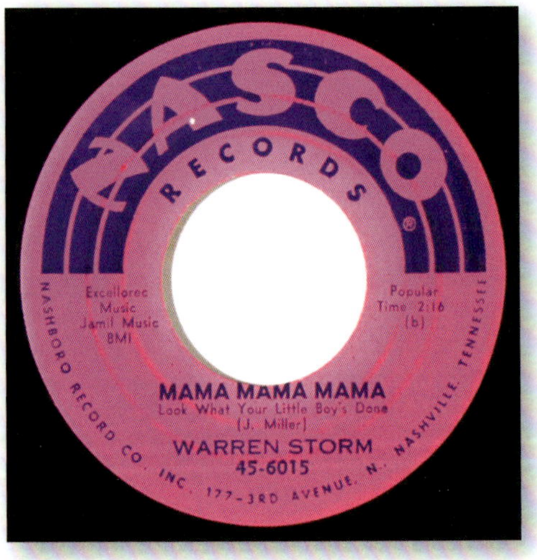

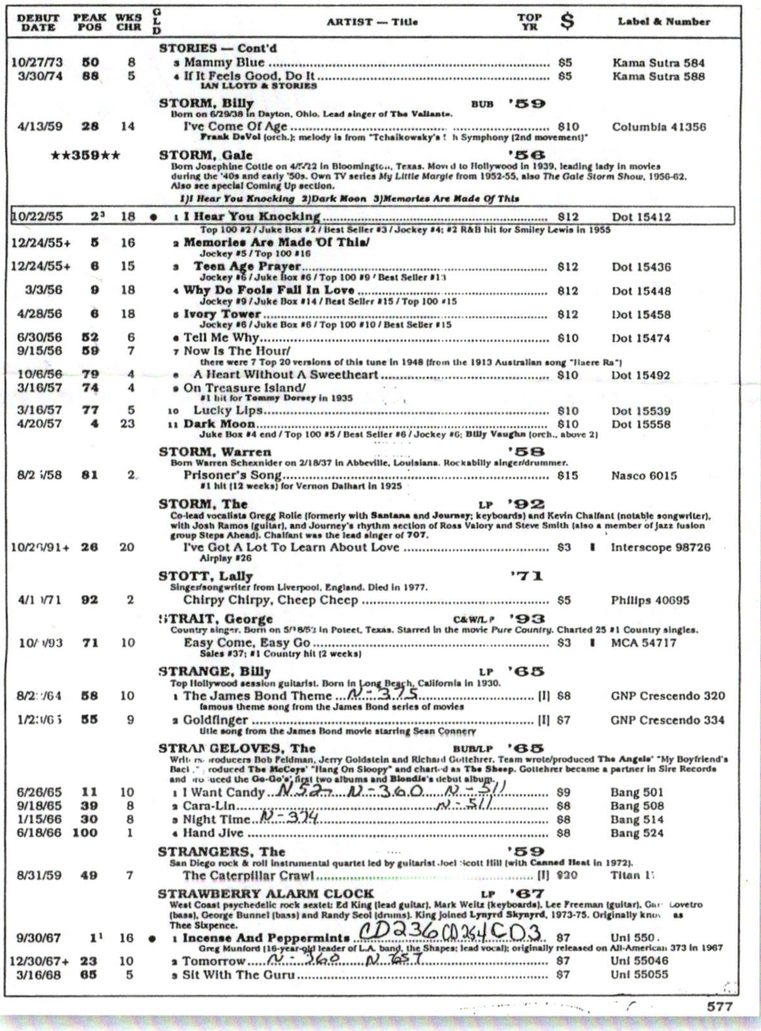

DEBUT DATE	PEAK POS	WKS CHR	GLD	ARTIST — Title	TOP YR	$	Label & Number
				STORIES — Cont'd			
10/27/73	50	8		3 Mammy Blue		$5	Kama Sutra 584
3/30/74	88	5		4 If It Feels Good, Do It IAN LLOYD & STORIES		$5	Kama Sutra 588
				STORM, Billy BUB Born on 6/29/38 in Dayton, Ohio. Lead singer of The Valiants.	'59		
4/13/59	28	14		I've Come Of Age Frank DeVol (orch.); melody is from "Tchaikowsky's [illegible]h Symphony (2nd movement)"		$10	Columbia 41356
	★★359★★			**STORM, Gale** Born Josephine Cottle on 4/5/22 in Bloomington, Texas. Moved to Hollywood in 1939, leading lady in movies during the '40s and early '50s. Own TV series *My Little Margie* from 1952-55, also *The Gale Storm Show*, 1956-62. Also see special Coming Up section. *1)I Hear You Knocking 2)Dark Moon 3)Memories Are Made Of This*	'56		
10/22/55	2^3	18	●	1 **I Hear You Knocking** Top 100 #2 / Juke Box #2 / Best Seller #3 / Jockey #4; #2 R&B hit for Smiley Lewis in 1955		$12	Dot 15412
12/24/55+	5	16		2 **Memories Are Made Of This/** Jockey #5 / Top 100 #16			
12/24/55+	6	15		3 **Teen Age Prayer** Jockey #6 / Juke Box #6 / Top 100 #9 / Best Seller #13		$12	Dot 15436
3/3/56	9	18		4 **Why Do Fools Fall In Love** Jockey #9 / Juke Box #14 / Best Seller #15 / Top 100 #15		$12	Dot 15448
4/28/56	6	18		5 **Ivory Tower** Jockey #6 / Juke Box #6 / Top 100 #10 / Best Seller #15		$12	Dot 15458
6/30/56	52	6		6 Tell Me Why		$10	Dot 15474
9/15/56	59	7		7 Now Is The Hour/ there were 7 Top 20 versions of this tune in 1948 (from the 1913 Australian song "Haere Ra")			
10/6/56	79	4		8 A Heart Without A Sweetheart		$10	Dot 15492
3/16/57	74	4		9 On Treasure Island/ #1 hit for Tommy Dorsey in 1935			
3/16/57	77	5		10 Lucky Lips		$10	Dot 15539
4/20/57	4	23		11 **Dark Moon** Juke Box #4 end / Top 100 #5 / Best Seller #6 / Jockey #6; Billy Vaughn (orch., above 2)		$10	Dot 15558
				STORM, Warren Born Warren Schexnider on 2/18/37 in Abbeville, Louisiana. Rockabilly singer/drummer.	'58		
> 8/25/58	81	2		Prisoner's Song #1 hit (12 weeks) for Vernon Dalhart in 1925		$15	Nasco 6015
				STORM, The LP Co-lead vocalists Gregg Rolie (formerly with Santana and Journey; keyboards) and Kevin Chalfant (notable songwriter), with Josh Ramos (guitar), and Journey's rhythm section of Ross Valory and Steve Smith (also a member of jazz fusion group Steps Ahead). Chalfant was the lead singer of 707.	'92		
10/26/91+	26	20		I've Got A Lot To Learn About Love Airplay #26		$3 ▮	Interscope 98726
				STOTT, Lally Singer/songwriter from Liverpool, England. Died in 1977.	'71		
4/10/71	92	2		Chirpy Chirpy, Cheep Cheep		$5	Philips 40695
				STRAIT, George C&W/LP Country singer. Born on 5/18/52 in Poteet, Texas. Starred in the movie *Pure Country*. Charted 25 #1 Country singles.	'93		
10/[illegible]/93	71	10		Easy Come, Easy Go Sales #37; #1 Country hit (2 weeks)		$3 ▮	MCA 54717
				STRANGE, Billy LP Top Hollywood session guitarist. Born in Long Beach, California in 1930.	'65		
8/2[illegible]/64	58	10		1 The James Bond Theme [I] famous theme song from the James Bond series of movies		$8	GNP Crescendo 320
1/2[illegible]/65	55	9		2 Goldfinger [I] title song from the James Bond movie starring Sean Connery		$7	GNP Crescendo 334
				STRANGELOVES, The BUB/LP Writers/producers Bob Feldman, Jerry Goldstein and Richard Gottehrer. Team wrote/produced The Angels' "My Boyfriend's Back," produced The McCoys' "Hang On Sloopy" and charted as The Sheep. Gottehrer became a partner in Sire Records and produced the Go-Go's' first two albums and Blondie's debut album.	'65		
6/26/65	11	10		1 I Want Candy		$9	Bang 501
9/18/65	39	8		2 Cara-Lin		$8	Bang 508
1/15/66	30	8		3 Night Time		$8	Bang 514
6/18/66	100	1		4 Hand Jive		$8	Bang 524
				STRANGERS, The San Diego rock & roll instrumental quartet led by guitarist Joel Scott Hill (with Canned Heat in 1972).	'59		
8/31/59	49	7		The Caterpillar Crawl [I]		$20	Titan 1[illegible]
				STRAWBERRY ALARM CLOCK LP West Coast psychedelic rock sextet: Ed King (lead guitar), Mark Weitz (keyboards), Lee Freeman (guitar), Gary Lovetro (bass), George Bunnel (bass) and Randy Seol (drums). King joined Lynyrd Skynyrd, 1973-75. Originally known as Thee Sixpence.	'67		
9/30/67	1^1	16	●	1 **Incense And Peppermints** Greg Munford (16-year-old leader of L.A. band, the Shapes; lead vocal); originally released on All-American 373 in 1967		$7	Uni 550[illegible]
12/30/67+	23	10		2 Tomorrow		$7	Uni 55046
3/16/68	65	5		3 Sit With The Guru		$7	Uni 55055

577

Record Research, Inc.

YL: What happened next?

WS: I continued recording with J.D. Miller up until 1979. I'd sign five years at a time.

YL: Why sign a contract for so long?

WS: A poor boy couldn't pay for the sessions, you know?

YL: Did you record all of those years at the same studio in Crowley?

In the mid-50s, while visiting my grandmother Cecile Broussard in Abbeville, Louisiana, I met Warren Schexnider while hanging around with my cousins and their friends. At the time, I don't know if Warren knew what a great career he would have in music. In 1958, his recording career began with his signature recording of "Prisoner's Song," and "Mama, Mama, Mama." Warren Storm has been a household name ever since. A host of drummers in South Louisiana and Southeast Texas wanted to play drums like Warren or at least try to copy his style. His vocals have always been outstanding and powerful with his very distinct voice. Through the years, Warren has always worked hard and sang his heart out. Few artists have recorded as much as Warren. He probably can't remember all the recording sessions he played drums on for other artists. Of course, as the song goes, "Warren is the Last Man Standing."

Proud to be a friend of The Great Warren Storm.

—JIVIN' GENE BOURGEOIS

WS: J.D. had four different studios in Crowley. He had one upstairs where the mayor's office is at now; they remodeled all that. Then he had another one, not far from there, and one at his house—so he had about four or five studios in the period of twenty-something years, I guess.

YL: Twenty-one years old, your first recording hit the *Billboard Charts*—how did Warren Storm feel?

WS: I felt pretty good then. [*laughs*] You know, I had a lotta gigs, and then in '58, when the "Prisoner's Song" came out, J.D. Miller flew me to Memphis. I did a TV show, it was like a mini *American Bandstand* where kids would dance and you'd lip-sync your song. Wink Martindale was the host. It was called *Wink Martindale Presents.* Back then Wink Martindale and Elvis Presley was very good friends. So, I did the TV show…Narvel Felts, that made "Reconsider Me," was on there by the way. He went after me.

WS: So anyway, Wink Martindale told me, he said, "Elvis is in town, would you like to meet him?" I said, "Well of course." So, before the show, he wrote me a note. I don't know what it said, but he handed it to me and said that I should go to the gate and present that to the guard.

YL: Were you alone at the time?

WS: No. A friend of mine from Abbeville flew with me to Memphis. His name is Stafford Palombo. He lives in Baton Rouge…he's rich now! [*laughs*] He's got a chemical company out there.

WS: After the show, I took the paper that Wink Martindale gave me, got a cab, and went to the mansion, Graceland. They had about forty people at the front gate, mostly girls.

WS: But anyway, that cab driver turned and said, "Y'all won't be able to go in there tonight. They got forty-something people at the gate that can't get in." So, I said, "OK," but told him to pull up to the gate anyway. I got down and presented that note to the guard. He took it, looked at it, and then got in his car and drove to the mansion. I guess he went in there and told Elvis. Elvis was in the house, at the piano, with about fifteen guests. They were having a little party. So, after a while, the car comes back to the gate. The guard said, "Open the gate." [*Warren laughs heartily*]

YL: No WAY!

WS: Hehehe, yeah! Them girls said, "Can we go? Can we go?" I said, "Noooo." So, me and Stafford got in the guard's car and he drove us to the mansion.

YL: What were you thinking/feeling at that point? You were about to meet Elvis!

WS: I remember saying, "We gonna meet the King, man!" That was in '58 before he became a huge, humongous, mega-star. But he was already a star. His first movie, *Love Me Tender,* was about to be released.

WS: So, anyway, we walked in the mansion, and I could see Elvis sitting at the piano. Elvis looked up and said, "Come sit at the piano." I sat on the piano stool, right next to him, and we talked.

WS: You not gonna believe this, man, he played a little bit of the "Prisoner's Song," because he had just seen me on the TV show! We stayed there for about an hour and talked about music and different things. I could see all the stuff that people would send him–stacks of drawings that people drew of him and art and all that stuff. We asked him where would be a good place to go after hours; he said, "Don't go to this one, don't go to that one, but you can go to that one." He knew all the places not to go, you know, to listen to music. And that was it. I said, "Well, can you give us a souvenir to take back? They not gonna believe this, them people back home." So that's when he autographed us each a picture.

YL: Did you sing together with him?

WS: No.

YL: Did Elvis sing while you were there?

WS: Yeah, he sang part of the "Prisoner's Song," but it was RATED X!

YL: What did Elvis sing?!

WS: It's XXX rated. Could I say that?

YL: Yes.

WS: [*singing and blushing*] "If I had the wings of an angel, and the balls of a hairy baboon, I'd climb to the top of the mountain, and cornhole the man in the moon."

WS: Could you believe that?! Elvis was funny man. [*laughs*]

YL: What was the most memorable thing that Elvis said?

WS: Well, he said, "I saw you on the show, and it was great. I liked it."

YL: The record was brand new when you went to Memphis. How long did it take before it charted at No. 81 on *Billboard*?

WS: I have no idea…a couple of weeks maybe?

WS: Now in 1959, I recorded four records on NASCO—eight songs. I recorded "Troubles, Troubles" [*sings*] "…troubles on my mind." It became No. 1 in Birmingham, Alabama. I did a show over there with Johnny Cash.

YL: You met Johnny Cash?

WS: Yes sir. And somebody took a picture of me and him. I still didn't have a camera! It was Johnny Cash, a bass player, and Luther on the guitar. Luther Perkins. That was Carl Perkins brother. Carl Perkins wrote "Blue Suede Shoes." Carl Perkins was there, but Luther, his brother, was playing guitar, right there with Johnny Cash. We did two shows at the National Guard Armory in 1959. I got a photo somewhere that shows that I was there… *The Johnny Cash Show featuring Warren Storm, Travis and Bob*. Travis and Bob was two guys that sang like the Everly Brothers.

YL: Was J.D. Miller the one who was booking all of these gigs for you?

WS: Yes. Yeah, he was. In fact, him and his wife drove me to Birmingham for that show.

YL: Did you bring a full band with you for that show?

WS: No, I played with musicians from out there. They had learned my song. All I did was one song.

[*Warren starts singing…"troubles on my mind…"*]

WS: Would you believe I had the No. 1 song and Johnny Cash's song was No. 2?! "Don't Take Your Guns to Town" was No. 2 in Birmingham.

YL: Were you married at the time?

WS: No, I didn't get married until 1960.

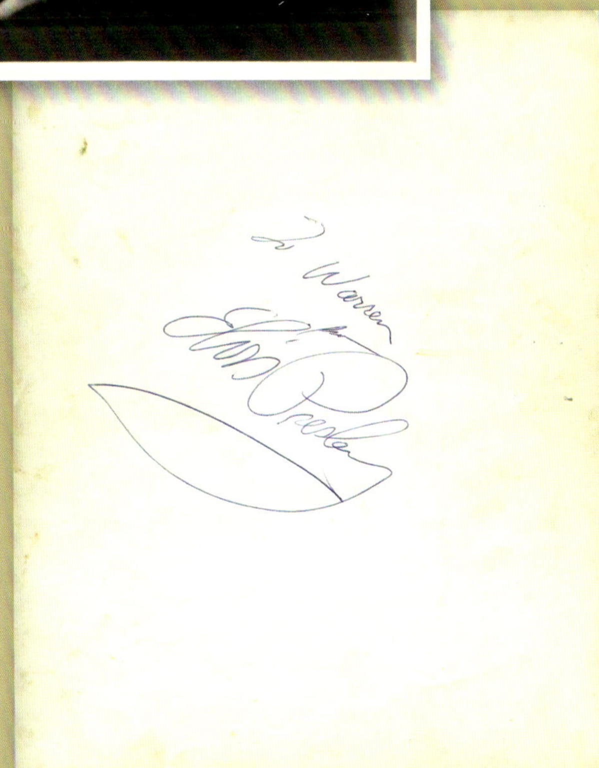

YL: In 1959, you recorded "Troubles, Troubles" on NASCO. What was on the other side?

WS: "In My Moments of Sorrow," I had another double hit. It didn't chart as high as my first one, but it hit No. 1 in Birmingham, Baton Rouge, and Houston.

YL: Did you receive any royalties for that hit?

WS: None. I made my money on personal appearances on this one. I never receive any royalties. [*laughing*] You see…I should be rich today…but I'm not.

YL: What shows did you do to promote "Troubles, Troubles"?

WS: I did a TV show with Mickey Gilley in Houston, in '59. [*laughs*]

YL: Micky Gilley?!

WS: I don't remember the name of the TV show. But I had been knowing Mickey Gilley since '58.

YL: Was it because of the NASCO record label in Nashville that allowed you to hook up with the likes of Mickey Gilley and Johnny Cash?

WS: Yes. That was a good year, man.

YL: What did you sing on the show?

WS: I just did "Troubles, Troubles," like the Birmingham thing.

YL: You said this was your follow up hit to the "Prisoner's Song," and it didn't chart as well nationally. How high did it go?

WS: Oh, it might have gone, maybe in the top 100…90 or something like that.

YL: Who were the musicians that recorded on this record?

WS: Local musicians from around Crowley, Lafayette, and me. I played drums on all of my recordings except when Jockey played drums on the "Prisoner's Song."

YL: Did you ever play guitar on any of the songs you recorded?

WS: [*laughs*] No. See, I only played guitar when the song had just three chords. Never more than three chords! That's all I knew.

YL: Did you bring a band up to Houston to do the show with Mickey Gilley?

WS: No. You just lip-synced those shows. I did some shows in New Orleans too.

Mickey Gilley and Warren Storm

Grant Clement, Warren Storm, Mickey Gilley, and Willie "Tee" Trahan (Branson, MO, 2015)

"Absolutely. I got more time than money, girl!"

WS: This was taken at the theatre in Branson, Missouri. Me and Mickey Gilley had known each other since 1958. We played bars and everything together. I went to Branson on a bus tour just to see what it was like over there, and Mickey said, "Warren, after the show come meet me backstage." We're that close.

WS: Oh, I forgot to tell you, I also did a show with Jimmy Donley. He was a great songwriter. Jim wrote seven songs for Fats Domino. He was a great singer too. We did the WWL TV show in New Orleans together in '58.

[*After a brief pause in the conversation, Warren looks up...*]

WS: Aw, this is gonna be so incredible! I told all my kids about this thing here, the book. They're excited!

YL: I'd like to ask you a few more questions before we call it a day. Are you good with that?

WS: "Absolutely. I got more time than money, girl!"

FEB 28, 1962

GRAND OPENING

OF

WHIT'S LOUNGE

Newly Remodeled and Decorated

UNDER NEW MANAGEMENT OF J. B. FONTENOT

ENTERTAINMENT BY RECORDING STAR

WARREN STORM & THE FOUR WINDS

Featuring Glen On the Organ

COCKTAIL HOUR DAILY FROM 4:30 P.M. to 6:30 P.M.

ALL MIXED DRINKS 35c

Plenty of Parking Area

Warren Storm & The Four Winds (1962)

YL: Let's talk more about your bands. After the Warren Storm Band and before you formed The Shondells, you had a band called Warren Storm & The Four Winds. Tell me about them.

WS: That's Bobby McBride on bass. Interesting story, Bobby didn't have a bass, so he would just play the top four strings like a bass guitar and not use the rest! Glen Guilbeau was on piano and Al Foreman played guitar. We didn't last long. That was just one of the things I put together.

WS: This gig was after they remodeled Whit's Lounge in 1962, but I played there in 1958.

YL: Tell me about The Shondells.

WS: There's Rod Bernard, he sang and played rhythm guitar, Skip Stewart sang and played bass, Sydney Janice played sax, Lewis Longlanais played sax too, Jessie Domingue was on lead guitar the first time, and Oscar Bernard played lead guitar the second time. And that's me on vocals and drums.

WS: See, in 1963, I was working in the printing department at the city hall in Lafayette. Rod Bernard and Skip Stewart came in and asked me if I wanted to play/start a band. I said, "Well, yes." I was just jobbing around, you know. That's when The Shondells started, in 1963, and we played all over Acadiana. At one time we were playing seven nights a week, well, eight nights a week…twice on Sundays. And we named that band Warren Storm, Rod Bernard, Skip Stewart and The Shondells.

YL: How did the name come about?

WS: Well, you know they had a nationwide band called The Shondells, so that's where we got it. Rod Bernard kind of stole it. [*laughing*]

WS: Also, Rod was working for Channel 10 at the time and we had a show called *The Saturday Hop*. Every Saturday we played an hour on TV.

WS: We worked a lot, that's for sure! Local clubs and all over the state of Louisiana.

YL: How did the band travel to the gigs?

WS: We had a wagon…well, I had a wagon. Everybody else would more or less go in their cars to the gigs.

YL: Were you in charge of bringing all of the equipment?

WS: Unfortunately, yes! I had my drums and the sound system and amplifiers. Yep, I had a station wagon.

YL: Was this a popular group?

WS: Yes. We were well known because of the TV show, I guess. And, we were all recording artists.

WS: It was a great band, we all got along, and we never had any drama…I was the only *druma*!

YL: Did you have a record with this band?

WS: We had one recording, *The Shondells at the Saturday Hop*. *At the Saturday Hop* was also the TV show that Rod had on Saturdays on Channel 10. We played there, live on TV.

The Shondells

The Shondells at the Saturday Hop *(La Louisiane Records, 1964)*

YL: Where did you record this album?

WS: At La Louisiane Recording Studio in Lafayette, Louisiana. After The Shondells, I just played with different groups. We lasted from 1963 to 1970–72, something like that. We had a good run.

YL: Any stories about the Shondells?

WS: During that time, The Beatles came out, so we had a little segment in our show where me and Jessie Domingue, Skip, and Rod got us some wigs. We'd dress up like The Beatles and we'd do a little segment of their songs! [*laughing*]

WS: Listen, we played at the Southern Club in Opelousas, Louisiana, and the people were standing on the chairs to see that happen! It was unbelievable! We'd do it every Saturday when we'd play at the Southern Club. They had about 600–700 people there.

YL: What made y'all do that?

WS: Well, we couldn't beat 'em, so we joined them!

YL: The Shondells were a swamp pop band?

WS: Absolutely.

YL: What's this annual reunion poster about?

WS: Of course, I played at the Southern Club for a long time, 1963 through the early 1970s. Then, in 1984, we decided to have a reunion. Mr. Chick Vidrine owned the Southern Club back then; he's long passed away, but he suggested it.

Rod Bernard, Warren Storm, Chick Vidrine, and Skip Stewart (1984)

Many years ago, I asked a super guitar picker friend of mine, Kenny Gill, to come with me to listen to a new band Warren Storm was forming. We went out to listen to Warren that night, and after about the third or fourth song, Kenny leaned over to me and said what I thought he would say: "Man, Warren Storm *is* the band! They wouldn't have a band without Warren Storm!" And I agreed with him.

The public doesn't give Warren the credit that he deserves, because only musicians realize the talent inside this man. He can sing anything. Ask him to sing a Cajun French song, he can do that. Ask him to sing a country-and-western song, he'll do it. Ask Warren to sing a rock 'n' roll song, he'll do that. Ask him to sing a blues song, he'll do that. It doesn't matter what type of music, what kind of music, whether it's Little Richard or Elvis Presley, Warren can sing them all, and not everybody can do that. He's one of a few who can do songs like that.

He's also very funny. He has his own sense of humor. One night at the Southern Club in Opelousas where we played, they were renovating the back of the club, and before the dance started, Warren came walking right down the middle of the floor carrying a door under his arm, saying, "OK, boys, tonight we're playing for the door." That would not be funny to most people, but to musicians it was hilarious. ["Playing for the door" means to perform for the money collected at a venue's entrance.] Another time I told him about these little pills we were taking that we thought were to lose weight, and I found out they were very addictive, and I told Warren, "Warren, you know those little pills we've been taking? Those things are very addictive." He said, "They're not, either." I said, "Yeah they are, Warren, you need to stop taking those things." He said, "They're not habit forming and I ought to know, I've been taking 'em for twenty years."

I'm very proud to know that I lived during an era when I knew Warren Storm, met Warren Storm, played music with Warren Storm for many, many years. We always had fun and had a great time. I've always admired him as a singer, a musician, a friend, and a gentleman. I'm just so glad that our paths in life crossed.

—Rod Bernard

WS: We were thinking about doing an annual reunion, but we only did a couple of them.

WS: Now the Southern Club is still standing…but barely. Just like Warren Storm…*barely standing*. [*laughing*] This is fun, huh?!

YL: You told me that your first language was French. Did you ever record anything in French?

WS: I recorded two French songs on a record called *Cajun Born* in 1989 [*starts singing*] "danse, danse, tite fille…" Johnnie Allan wrote that song.

YL: Can you translate for those who don't speak French?

WS: Dance, dance, little girl (in the arms of another…).

WS: I was a guest on the recording session. Me, Johnnie Allan, and Clint West. I sang two Cajun songs in French, "Danse, Danse Tite Fille," and the "House with Two Doors" ("La Maison à Deaux Portes"). Which was a great album. It's on La Louisiane. It was only on an LP and cassette tape.

YL: When you sang swamp pop tunes, did you ever sign them in French?

WS: No…strictly in English.

YL: Before we go back to the 1950s when you were a studio drummer recording with Lazy Lester, Slim Harpo, and Lonesome Sundown, I'd like to ask just a few more questions about your childhood.

WS: My daddy was a sharecropper and we got to live on the land for free as long as he worked for the man that owned the land. We had hogs and chickens. My daddy basically worked for a place to live. He made extra money playing music.

Far left: Warren Storm's first communion

Left: Warren Storm (Stunt Night, Abbeville High School, 1956)

YL: Did you go to church as a family?

WS: No. We weren't churchgoers, but I made my first communion. That was a must back then.

WS: When we moved to Abbeville, they had more homes there. We weren't as far out in the country. But the homes in Abbeville were about a half-mile away. We were surrounded by rice fields.

YL: How did you get around in those days?

WS: We had a buggy and a wagon and a horse to pull it. I never rode the horse itself, just the buggy. Later, when I was ten or twelve years old, my daddy had a car. It was an old Ford or Chevy, I don't remember which. I didn't get to drive until I was nineteen! You know, I'd work with different bands and they'd pick me up.

YL: You said that times were hard growing up. What was the best part of growing up?

WS: The best part of growing up was playing music. That's what I wanted to do.

YL: What was the worst part of growing up?

WS: [*without hesitation*] Going to school! [*laughs*] Because, it was hard. I had difficulties learning in school. But I did make it to the twelfth grade and graduated.

YL: Did you play any kind of sports in school?

WS: No ma'am. No sports. I played in the varsity band in my last year in high school. That was my first time in the band, my senior year.

YL: Did you sing in high school choir?

WS: We had some little pageants in high school and I'd play the guitar or drums. "Stunt Night," they'd call it, and everybody would have a skit.

YL: Who painted the logo on your drums?

WS: I went to an artist in Abbeville. I got the logo from Gene Krupa. He had the "GK" on his drums. I just made mine "WS."

YL: I wanted to ask you about Cajun music and your family heritage. Have you traced your lineage?

WS: They came from Canada, I believe.

YL: Did you and your family listen to and/or play Cajun music?

WS: No. We didn't listen to Cajun music. We listened to what they called hillbilly music, which was country.

YL: You said you were not influenced by Cajun music. But your father had an accordion.

WS: I enjoyed listening to him play the accordion, and I did go listen to some Cajun musicians when I was about ten years old. I heard Joe Falcon. He was playing at some night club not far from Maurice. We went to the dance in a wagon. There was about five or six of us, family members, that piled into the wagon and went to the dance. I stood by the bandstand and I enjoyed it. That's a long time ago…I remember that though.

YL: Did you ever have the desire to play Cajun music?

WS: Well, I didn't play with no Cajun band growing up. They had a fiddle, guitar, upright bass, and drums, that's it. I started in my dad's band and that's what they had.

YL: So, Cajun music did not affect your playing or singing style?

WS: Not early on, but later it did. I played some Cajun music in the 1970s. I played at an old club on the Breaux Bridge Highway, it was called… what was it called before it was Boo Boo's Night Club? Right there in the vicinity of the Breaux Bridge Highway? Oh, The Midway Club. It was me, Rufus Thibodeaux, Tony Thibodeaux, Rodney Miller, and Jo-El Sonnier. I played drums. We played a year there. We didn't have a band name, we were just an all-star Cajun band. I did that on the side. One day out of the week, which was a Sunday afternoon, I'd play with them. But, I was still playing swamp pop with my other band.

YL: How did that come to be? Did you play with them just because it was another day to play music?

WS: They asked me to play, and that was part of my living, so while I was off, I played with them.

YL: And did you enjoy that gig?

WS: Oh, absolutely! I'd get a chance to sing some of my songs I recorded too.

YL: As a drummer, do you find Cajun music boring?

WS: No, not really. I enjoyed it. It's either a two-step or a waltz, but you know…[*laughing*]

YL: So why do you think you gravitated more toward the hillbilly/country music than Cajun music?

Cajun All Stars (1975)
Top row: Rodney Miller, Warren Storm, and Rufus Thibodeaux
Bottom row: Tony Thibodeaux, Jo-el Sonnier, and Gerald Romero
(Courtesy of La Louisianne)

WS: Because that's what was popular in the 1940s and 50s. Cajun music wasn't, but it is now!

WS: Then when I heard Fats Domino in 1953, I knew I wanted to play that kind of music. It was more of a drum kind of music.

WS: I remember I did an interview when Fats passed away, and I said, "If it wouldn't have been for Fats Domino, we wouldn't have no swamp pop."

YL: Who coined the term "swamp pop"?

WS: John Broven, a writer from England, came down and interviewed musicians around here. After hearing the music, he termed it "swamp pop." But it originated with Fats Domino, Little Richard, Chuck Berry...rhythm and blues. Some called it rock-n-roll, but, down in Louisiana, they called it swamp pop. It's really *Louisiana* rock-n-roll with a touch of rhythm and blues. You know...Fais Do Do meets Fats Domino.

YL: Let's go back to the 1950s when you were at Jay Miller's Studio in Crowley.

WS: I was a staff drummer for all of the old blues men that came in there. We'd stay a week at a time and record them. There was Lazy Lester and Katie Webster. She played the piano and sang on my recordings and I played on her recordings. Then they had Lightening Slim, Slim Harpo, Lonesome Sundown, that was all blues artist from Louisiana that came through there in the early 1950s and 1960s.

YL: So, you went into Jay Miller's studio as a singer and...

WS: And I ended up being a singer *and* a staff drummer.

YL: Do you know how many albums you recorded as a staff drummer?

WS: I'd say around twenty or so. Twenty artists came through there. They all were a big influence to me. I'd pick up something from each one that came through. All that soul that I got, comes from all those old blues men.

"Some called it rock-n-roll, but, down in Louisiana, they called it swamp pop. It's really Louisiana rock-n-roll with a touch of rhythm and blues. You know... Fais Do Do meets Fats Domino."

WS: That's why people from all over the world come here and want to stay. We got the best music, the best food...and it's 'cause we got soul.

YL: Our friend, Herman Fuselier, had an interesting question for you. He asked, "During this time when you were recording with all of these blues artists, segregation was the law of the land and the civil rights movement was brewing outside. How did you do it?"

WS: It might have been segregated on the outside, but not the musicians. We were like family. You know, one time, I brought Lazy Lester to the Forrest Club and he had to stay on the bandstand. He couldn't go down! That's what it was like on the outside of the studio.

WS: But inside, I never had any problems with that. We played together in the studios and we did dance jobs together.

YL: When you were recording at J. Miller Studio and you'd walk through the door, or these blues guys would walk through the door, everything was equal?

WS: Yes. You see, I always said, music has no color. That was exactly what happened.

YL: Do you think they felt the same way?

WS: I think so. I was the only white musician in there. We're just human beings, you know. We didn't even think about that. We were there to make music.

YL: Did your fans look at you differently or say anything because you were recording with these blues artists?

WS: Nope. We were fortunate, because musicians always had it good with other musicians, no matter what color. So that was a great thing, I mean you know, we just lived our lives and played music together. There was no color. None of that mattered.

WS: I wish the rest of the world could take an example from musicians. We're all friends. Music can save the world!

YL: When did you do your first radio show?

WS: In 1958, when the "Prisoner's Song" came out. I did it in Crowley. KSIG was right by the recording studio. "Mama, Mama, Mama" and the "Prisoner's Song," that's what got me to Memphis on the *Wink Martindale Show*, which got me to meet Elvis.

WS: Now after The Shondells, I went play with Rodney Miller and them. That Cajun band I told you about. I did a year with them.

WS: Then, in the 1970s, I started Warren Storm and The Bad Weather Band. After that, in the early 1980s, me and Willie "Tee" Trahan started our Cypress Band.

YL: Tell me about The Bad Weather band.

WS: Well, I had several Bad Weather bands. Originally, there was Grant Clement on guitar, Randy Barras on steel guitar, Percy Bernard on sax, George "Muscle" Bellot on bass, and I played drums. Then in 1974, we had Howard Foreman on sax, myself on drums, Jessie Credeur on steel guitar, and Hilton Falcon on bass. We were a five-piece band. We recorded one album in 1974.

YL: You said that Hilton Falcon played bass, but the name on the back of the picture is Joe Hill.

WS: Well, that's cause they're one in the same! I gave him that name. You see, he started writing and recording songs, so I told him, "I got a good name for you…Joe Hill." And he kept it!

Warren Storm and The Bad Weather Band (1974)

WS: Lord have mercy!

WS: You know, I recorded my first LP with that band.

YL: You had never recorded an LP before?

WS: Nope. Just singles. The title was *Warren Storm and Bad Weather*. I used studio musicians on this album. I didn't do it with the band that I was playing the gigs with.

YL: Why did you make the decision not to use your regular musicians?

WS: Hmmm...I don't know why, but I know I played drums on all those recordings.

WS: I was signed with J.D. Miller at the time. Possibly it was his decision to use studio musicians.

YL: Did you guys get along?

WS: You know, I always get along with musicians. I could go back sixty years and the musicians that worked with me then would still work with me today. That's because I treated everybody real good. We used to split all the money back then, equally you know. Take out expenses and then split it equally.

YL: When you were with The Bad Weather band, who was booking the gigs for you?

WS: I was, but I no longer do that, it's too much of a headache. And back then, we didn't have the technology that we have now on those smart phones. We had just a regular phone! A home number, you know.

YL: How did you promote the gigs? Did you have to do it yourself?

WS: Well, the clubs would get spots on the radio, I guess. We just got well-known, that's all. We were fortunate. It's not at all like we are today, because we didn't have that technology. They had a lot of clubs back then and word-of-mouth got around that we played here and there, but now all our clubs disappeared. Nowadays we just play festivals and casinos, when we can.

YL: When did The Bad Weather band disband?

WS: I think around 1979, something like that.

YL: Were you living here, in Broussard, when that happened?

WS: No. You see, I lived in six different places throughout my life, mostly in Lafayette. I lived on the Breaux Bridge Highway, and on Holly Street one time, then on Garfield Street, right in midtown Lafayette. Then, we bought a house on Pinhook and lived there for thirty-something years. Then we moved and I lived in a trailer in Lafayette Parish, and then I came to this apartment in Broussard thirty years ago.

YL: That's too many years! You're not that old!

WS: [*laughing*] I'm 102!

YL: What happened for Bad Weather to disband?

WS: Well, we just ran out of gigs. Everybody went play with different groups.

YL: After Bad Weather disbanded, what happened next?

WS: I played around with different groups, sitting in as a guest.

YL: Who was your favorite band to sit in with?

WS: Oh man, I had a lot of them. All the musicians in South Louisiana are all great. Everybody was good. I loved them all.

WS: There was this one group though, that I played with all over Louisiana and east Texas. We did the *Freddy Fender Show*, which was a CBS show. CBS Records would put on a show at Mickey Gilley's place in Pasadena, Texas. Freddy Fender, myself, and Tommy McLain did the show. We were all signed with CBS records that year. It wasn't really a band, we were just individual artists all recording for Huey Meaux out of Houston, Texas, in the mid-seventies...until 1979, actually.

YL: How'd you meet Freddy Fender?

WS: Well, my Bad Weather band backed up Freddy Fender when he was booked in South Louisiana. We backed him up for a lot of gigs. Freddy would just bring his guitar and sing. We took care of the rest. At the Southern Club and all over the place... Signorelli's in St. Martinville...we did a lot of shows with Freddy. He was a good friend.

WS: That's what Chuck Berry did all his life! He'd go from city to city and bring his guitar and local bands would back him up. He would just plug in his guitar and say, "Let's do it!" You see everybody knew his songs.

WS: I also played drums on one of Freddy's LPs in 1979. It was called *Freddy Fender Swamp Gold* and I have the LP here.

WS: That's me right there sitting on Freddy Fender's lap! We recorded that at Sugar Hill Studio in Houston, Texas. I played drums on all of the songs on the record.

Freddy Fender Recording Session (Sugar Hill Studios, Houston, TX, 1979)

YL: In the seventy years that you've played music, is there one gig that sticks out more than the rest? I understand it's a hard question to answer.

WS: Yes, it *is* a hard question. Well, it was really a great gig when we played at Gilley's in Pasadena, Texas. They had 5,000 people there. You can't ask for any better than that! That was back in 1978 and 1979, early 1980s. In the heyday, when Gilley's was rocking!

WS: And of course, throughout the years, since 1984, I did the Jazz Festival in New Orleans almost every year. And that's always a great gig.

NO AUDIO
OR VIDEO

New Orleans Jazz & Heritage Festival (1984)

WS: Look at that picture! The New Orleans Jazzfest, 1984. That's how long I've been playing there. That was Johnnie Allan's band in that picture. Nolan Cormier was playing the accordion. They had Van Broussard, Jivin' Gene back there you can't really see him, Johnnie Allan, Rod Bernard, Warren Storm, and Grace Broussard and Frankie Ford. I don't know who was playing bass.

Paul Simon and Warren Storm
(New Orleans Jazz & Heritage Festival)

Lloyd Price and Warren Storm
(New Orleans Jazz & Heritage Festival, 2002)

Warren Storm and John Goodman
(New Orleans Jazz & Heritage Festival, 2003)

YL: Did you meet any famous people throughout the years at Jazzfest?

WS: Yes! That's Paul "*See-Maw…*" Paul Simon, but we called him "*See-Maw,*" the French pronunciation. He used to hang out in Cecilia, Louisiana, a lot.

YL: Really?

WS: Yes! That's Dickie Landry's good friend!

WS: And I took this picture with John Goodman. You know he went out with a girl from New Orleans. He's a big man! He was backstage listening to our show. It must have been about twelve years ago, or something like that. No, it was 2003. The years, they go by fast!

WS: This is Lloyd Price. He was at the New Orleans Jazzfest with me. He recorded hundreds of songs like "Personality," and "Just Because." He was the first artist to do "Just Because." That was a swamp pop song.

YL: Was he a Louisiana native?

WS: I think he was from New Orleans originally, but he moved east to Philadelphia, or somewhere out there. But he recorded all of his famous songs in New Orleans.

WS: Then there were a lot of local legends.

Warren Storm and Ben Sandmel
(New Orleans Jazz & Heritage Festival)

Terry Huval, Warren Storm, Tommy Richard, and Willie "Tee" Trahan
(New Orleans Jazz & Heritage Festival)

Warren Storm, D.L. Menard, and Willie "Tee" Trahan
(New Orleans Jazz & Heritage Festival)

Rob Savoy, Warren Storm, and Willie "Tee" Trahan
(New Orleans Jazz & Heritage Festival)

Warren Storm (Blues Estafette, Utrecht, Holland, November 1991, Photos by Paul Harris)

[*Warren pauses for a second…*]

WS: Another favorite gig was one that I did in Holland. I played with a band from there. They had rehearsed all of my material and knew it just like the record. I asked them, "Are you sure y'all aren't from Louisiana?"

WS: A Dutch band...can you believe?! They had two horns; they had the whole thing. And I played the drums with them. I did that Holland festival for five years. It was called the Blues Estafete, in Utrecht. It's no longer in existence, but I did it five years in a row.

YL: How did you get a gig in Holland?

WS: I got the gig through some producers out of New Orleans and Chicago. George Paulus, who did my blues CD in Chicago, helped get me that gig. George passed away a couple of years ago.

WS: I met George at the Ponderosa Stomp in New Orleans. He saw me play drums with different musicians, got my number, called me, and flew me to Chicago to record.

WS: That was my first blues CD I recorded.

YL: Was this on NASCO Records?

WS: No, this was not on NASCO, this was on George Paulus's record company, in 2002. See, I went to Chicago five different times. I recorded with rockabilly artists that were on Sun Records years ago, I don't remember their names, but that's how I got to go to Chicago the first time, and eventually Holland.

YL: What was the title of your blues album?

WS: *Dust My Blues*. It's on a CD. I wasn't able to make an LP, only a CD. And I have that CD!

YL: Were you playing blues music at the time?

WS: No. George just sent me those tunes that he wanted me to do. He flew me up there to Chicago. He knew I had played the drums with all those old blues singers. We were only four musicians on the album. We had an upright bass, and Studebaker John, he was one of the premier harmonica and guitar players in Chicago, was on there too. He travels in a band with only two musicians, all over the United States, and plays.

WS: This was in 2002, the blues album. Fourteen songs–some new, some old. It was blues, Cajun, and rockabilly.

YL: Did he pay you to go up and make that record?

WS: Yes, he paid me. He gave me an advance of a couple of thousand dollars and a plane ticket. I stayed there for about a week.

YL: Did you ever get royalties on the record you recorded there?

WS: Well, I'd buy the CDs at cost and sell them at the gigs. That's how I made my money, and he gave me an advance to go out there, but no mailbox money.

WS: He'd pay me for the sessions when I'd go back and record with different rockabilly artists.

YL: How long did you freelance until you started the Cypress Band?

WS: Until the early 1980s. That's when we started the *first* Cypress Band.

YL: First?

WS: Yes. There's actually TWO Cypress Bands! Warren Storm, Willie Tee, and Cypress Bands. The first one lasted about ten or twelve years, then everybody went their different ways and played with different groups. Then thirteen years ago, we reformed the Cypress Band. And that's where I'm at today, with the Warren Storm, Willie Tee, and Cypress. We back up different artists and play theaters, like the Strand Theatre in Jennings. We have different guests come sit in like T.K. Hulin, Jivin' Gene, Tommy McLain, and Charlene Howard. We do different swamp pop shows all around Louisiana.

YL: Who was in the original Cypress Band?

WS: We passed through a lot of piano players and musicians. But originally, I think I have the picture that has the names on the back.

WS: Let's see if I can remember...1984 there was me, the guitar player, his nickname was "Boudin," his real name was Mark Seymour and...whew, I can't remember their names!

WS: We had a guy from North Carolina that played the bass. We had a sax, bass, piano, guitar, and drums. I can't remember their names right now, ain't that something!

I have so much respect for Warren Storm. Every single time that I have got to walk on stage with him, much less sing with him, I have considered it one of the most absolute highest honors and privileges that I have had in my music career. Not only do I have the utmost respect for all that he has accomplished in his music years, I admire his willingness to encourage people, myself included, and I particularly love that Warren is the same every time you see him. No pretentiousness, no attitudes, just a good guy!

—CHARLENE HOWARD

Cypress Band (Texas)

Original Cypress Band

WS: Let's see… [*left photo*] that's me, Warren Storm, on vocals and drums, Mark Seymour on guitar, Chet Blackstone on piano, unknown (bassist), and Willie "Tee" Trahan on sax.

WS: This is another configuration of the Cypress Band [*above photo*], Kyle Dugas on drums, Carl Bordelon on piano and trumpet, Willie "Tee" Trahan on sax and vocals, Warren Storm on vocals, Tommy Richard on guitar, and Gerald Romero on bass guitar.

WS: [*opposite page*] This time it's Scott Broussard on bass, Karl Dugas on drums, Warren Storm on vocals, Willie "Tee" Trahan on sax and vocals, Tommy Richard on guitar, and Carl Bordelon on piano and trumpet.

YL: Who is in the Cypress Band now?

WS: Well there's me on vocals, Willie Tee on sax, Tommy Richard on guitar, Carl Bordelon on piano, Larry Badon on bass, and Carl Dugas on drums.

YL: Do you ever rehearse?

WS: No. I've been rehearsing for seventy years! I'm so fortunate to still be doing this.

YL: How'd you get the idea to do the TV show?

WS: Well, Charlie Chatlain owned the station and he had the idea. Bill Besson and Charles started talking and they said, "Why don't y'all do a TV show?" And that's how we got started.

YL: Tell me about the show. I don't remember seeing it.

WS: Well, we had a little theme song, then when they'd come to me, I'd say, "This is Warren Storm, Willie Tee and the Cypress Band," and we'd start playing, just like on the bandstand.

YL: What was the name of the theme song?

WS: "Walking with Mr. Lee." It was an instrumental.

[*Warren starts humming the song...*]

YL: You must be doing something right, Warren. You're still packing the house!

WS: Well...

YL: How did you meet Willie Tee?

WS: Oh, we knew each other for a long time. We even worked at Romero's Music Store in Lafayette on Jefferson Street. I was working there and Willie was working with different bands, Clint West and everybody, so we decided to start our own band in 1980. Then in 1982, we had our own TV show on Channel 15. The name of the show was *Warren Storm, Willie Tee, and The Cypress Band.* That lasted two years, every Saturday. We'd tape on Monday nights. We'd tape four shows and that would last a whole month. They'd air the show on Saturdays. It was a thirty-minute show. I was the host. I wanted Bill Besson, the local TV personality for Channel 10, to host, but he said, "No, you go ahead and do it."

As a kid, I remember watching Warren Storm on TV. He was so cool! He was the first drummer I saw that was the front man. Warren and his drum kit were out front and he was large and in charge. The cat did it all. Warren has played it all. His career has spanned decades and he's always conformed to every genre of music that was hot at that time. He's always been able to re-invent himself in order to stay on top. Warren is blues. Warren is country. Warren is soul. Most of all, Warren Storm is the godfather of swamp pop!

When I wrote Warren's latest hit, "Last Man Standing," I didn't realize that I would put him under so much pressure. Now he stands onstage at gigs and everywhere he goes. Warren...you can sit down!

—Gumbo Phil Daigle

From left to right: David Ranson, David Greely, Pat Breaux, Warren Storm, Steve Riley, David Egan, Richard Comeaux, Dickey Landry (kneeling), and C.C. Adcock (sitting) (1998)

Lil' Band O' Gold Era

WS: We did that thing thousands of times! We still have the video tapes of it on VHS. Now, this Cypress Band lasted ten years. Then after, we started the Lil' Band O' Gold band. But, I was still playing with my Cypress Band. Man, that was hard.

YL: Why was it difficult?

WS: It was hard to rotate and keep the schedules straight.

YL: Name the musicians in this picture for me.

WS: That's David Ranson on bass, David Greely and Pat Breaux on sax, Warren Storm on drums, Steve Riley on accordion, David Egan on piano, Richard Comeaux on pedal steel guitar, Dickey Landry on sax, and C.C. Adcock on guitar. A bunch of us sang.

WS: This is when we were in Nice, France.

Dicky Landry, John Troutman, Warren Storm, Steve Riley, C.C. Adcock, Matthew Wilkinson, and David Egan (Cannes Film Festival, Nice, France, 2009)

YL: What were you doing in France? Were you performing?

WS: This was when they previewed our movie there, *Promised Land*. Look the red carpet! All them big stars were there previewing their movies.

YL: Tell me about this movie. Who decided to make a documentary about Lil' Band O' Gold?

WS: Well, Lil' Band O' Gold went into La Louisiane studio and we recorded an album called *The Promised Land*. I think the record company for that album decided to make a documentary. They filmed while we were recording it. The documentary is called *The Promised Land–A Swamp Pop Journey*. That was in 2009.

YL: How long did it take to film the movie?

WS: Matthew Wilkinson, that's the one that filmed it. He's from France. He'd do a little bit every day. He spent the week there with us. Then he came along with us when we played in Texas. I'd tell him, "Get that camera out of my face, boy!" [*laughing*]

WS: He traveled with us and was with us twenty-four hours a day. I remember when Harriet cooked outside of the studio, he filmed that too.

YL: So not only are you the "Godfather of Swamp Pop," you're a movie star too?

WS: Aw well...that's what they say. But the film wasn't released in the states. It was only released overseas. I wish it would have been in the states, man. But we previewed it over here in the theaters in Lafayette, New Orleans, and Baton Rouge.

YL: How did Lil' Band O' Gold get started?

WS: Back in 1998, I think, Steve Riley and C.C. Adcock, two local musicians, came see me one night when I was singing at the Four Seasons Club. I sang there with another band every night. The first Four Seasons was on Johnston Street, and the

I had the pleasure of playing with Warren in the mid-90s with Lil' Band O' Gold. Instantly, we became like brothers. We were roommates on the road, and yes, there were many laughs!

I've never played with a more soulful drummer. Warren was always "in the pocket," too! His singing was always spot on. His vocal range was incredible!

Thank you for all of the fond memories, my brother.

Love you always,

—RICHARD "T-COE" COMEAUX

second one was on West Congress. So anyway, C.C. Adcock and Steve Riley would come in to listen to me play. They'd come in all the time. Their favorite song was "Seven Letters."

YL: What configuration were you with at that time?

WS: It was just a bunch of musicians that got together. I think we were just The Warren Storm Band. There was Kenny Tibbs on bass and vocals, Carl Dugas on drums, Gerald Bernard on guitar, and then different keyboard players would come sit in.

WS: So, one night, C.C. and Steve started talking to me about playing music with them. They said, "Look, we're jamming on Monday nights at the Swamp Water Saloon." That place is no longer there. It was on Bertrand Drive in Lafayette. Anyway, they wanted me to go jam with them, but I had quit playing drums. I hadn't really played them for eight or ten years. I was just singing at the time.

YL: Why had you quit playing drums?

WS: Because it had become too hard. I had played for fifty years. When you get old, you know, the wear and tear on your bones...it was a physical thing. My mind wanted to play, but my body just couldn't do it.

WS: Anyway, they wanted me to go jam on Monday nights. They almost begged me to go. I said, "I don't play drums anymore." They said, "Well, come jam anyway."

WS: So, one Monday night, I went. Richard Comeaux (pedal steel guitar ace from Breaux Bridge) was there. Basically, that's how the Lil' Band O' Gold got started. I jammed with them one Monday night, and thirteen years later, I was still playing with them.

WS: I said, "You see what y'all made me do?!"

YL: But you told me you couldn't physically play drums anymore.

WS: You know, when I played with the Lil' Band O' Gold, we did a lot of festivals and they always furnished the drums, so I didn't have to roadie or nothing like that. And gigs were short, 45 minutes or so. It wasn't like I had to haul my drums and play a three- or four-hour gig. So, it worked out.

YL: This was a very popular band with some pretty distinguished musicians. Did you guys play mostly local gigs?

WS: We traveled all over the United States from the East Coast to the Midwest to the West Coast and all over the world. I was just fortunate to be able to do that.

YL: Did you record with Lil' Band O Gold?

WS: Yes. We recorded at a studio in New Orleans. I recorded on all three records, *The Promised Land* (2011), *Lil' Band O' Gold* (2000), and *Plays Fats* (2012).

YL: Did you enjoy traveling?

WS: Yes, but I'm not traveling anymore. It would be too hard.

YL: Hmmm…Lil' Band O' Gold, on the road…I'm sure there are some funny stories. Fess up.

WS: Well, I'm sure you've heard a bunch of them anyway, but some of those stories are rated X! [*laughing*]

WS: XXX! [*laughing harder*]

YL: You can tell the stories Warren, we don't have to put them in the book…

WS: No, no. I'm not going to say anything.

YL: There was kind of a rift in the universe when Lil' Band O' Gold quit playing–a shock felt round the world, so to speak. What really happened? There's a lot of speculation. Was it a nasty breakup?

WS: Well, it wasn't nasty, they just didn't want me to quit.

YL: Why did you want to quit?

WS: Because, I had had enough of juggling two bands and dates. It was driving me crazy, man. Plus, we started playing dances around here and those gigs were three hours long.

WS: For three months they hassled me man, and I said, "Look. I'm not playing drums anymore. It's too hard. Can't y'all get that?" But they had some bookings and they wanted me to honor those, but I just couldn't do it.

WS: But it's all good now. We're all friends.

"My mind wanted to play, but my body just couldn't do it."

YL: We've talked about some pretty memorable times so far. What do you think was the best Warren Storm musical moment?

WS: Lord have mercy!

WS: You know, the best moment is every moment. Any time I can perform, and get on the bandstand, and make the people happy and dance, that's it. That's the best moment! Like when I sing with Yvette Landry. [*laughing*]

YL: Tell me about these pictures from your travels with Lil' Band O' Gold.

Opposite: Warren Storm (Lincoln Center, New York City, 2000)

Right: Warren Storm (New York City)

Bottom right: Richard Comeaux, Warren Storm, and Pat Breaux (New York City, 2002)

WS: That's in New York City. See the Twin Towers in the back? We were there before the Towers went down. They're not there no more.

WS: Can you believe, that was nineteen years ago?

WS: This was in New York too, at the Lincoln Center. We played outside. We toured the East Coast, the Midwest, and the West. We leased a bus in Lafayette and drove up the East Coast. After a couple of months, we flew to other venues. Our first gig of the tour was in Annapolis, Maryland.

Lil' Band O' Gold
(London, England, 2007)

Top: Warren Storm and Jay Jackson

Bottom: Jack Ross on bass and Leo Jackson on rhythm guitar

YL: What type of venues did you play on tour?

WS: It was mostly festivals.

YL: Do you prefer playing festivals or bars?

WS: I like the clubs, you know, where you can get close to the people.

YL: Let's go back to 1984. You went up to Nashville and recorded your *Heart and Soul* album. Was that recorded with studio musicians?

[*Warren pulls out a photo album from when he recorded at Owen Bradley's Studio in Nashville. He starts flipping through, lost in memories.*]

WS: Yes. I was playing with the original Willie Tee and Cypress Band, but didn't record with them.

YL: What musicians did you use to record?

WS: I used the Nashville Sound studio band. They recorded with the Everly Brothers, Brenda Lee, and everybody. They were just a great studio band. They had Floyd Cramer, Boots Randolph, Grady Martin, and Hank Garland on the guitar, Buddy Harman on the drums, and Bobby Moore on the bass.

YL: Floyd Cramer recorded with you?

WS: Absolutely. I did four songs for Top Rank Records out of New York, and only two were released on that session.

YL: What two songs were released?

WS: "No No," which J.D. Miller wrote, and "The Bohawk Georgia Grind." It was supposed to be like a new dance they invented, you know.

YL: Did the songs or the dance catch on?

WS: No. Top Rank Records was a major label, but after they released my two songs, they went out of business.

YL: Did you put them out of business, Warren?

WS: Probably did. [*laughing*] That was all the luck I had. I have a 45 of that record though.

WS: I remember, I recorded in the afternoon, and Brenda Lee recorded before me. They had two levels in the studio, bottom and top. She recorded at the top before me with the same band! After they finished her session, they came down and did my session.

YL: Did you meet Brenda Lee?

WS: Nope, I wish I would have, but I never did. What an artist, huh? But her band and my band were one in the same on the recordings.

YL: How did the members of the Cypress Band feel about you going up to Nashville and recording a record without them?

WS: Well, I just went for four days. They just played without me, you know. They got another drummer for those four days.

YL: Are you saying that they were supportive of you going make this record?

WS: Absolutely. They were really supportive.

WS: You see the more famous *I* got, the more gigs *we* got. [*laughing*] It's a simple thing, right?!

> Warren has a great voice and style that is unique, and only Warren. No one can copy him. He knows what his audience wants and always delivers. He is truly a nice guy and a great friend.
>
> —T. K. Hulin

Warren Storm and Bob Hendricks in Nashville

YL: Were you nervous to record on those sessions?

WS: No, I wasn't nervous, I was thrilled. Those musicians there made me feel like they knew me forever.

YL: Who initially got you to do this session?

WS: Bob Hendricks. He had an art store and he would frame stuff for recording artists. I was recording for Huey Meaux at the time, but Bob came down and got a release from him so I could go and record that album.

YL: How did Bob Hendricks know about you?

WS: Through Eddy Raven. One day, Eddy walked into Bob's store to get something framed. Bob was playing my song, "So Long, So Long," on his record player, and Eddy said, "That sounds like Warren Storm." Bob said, "That is! You know him?" Eddy said, "Yes. He's from my hometown, Lafayette. He played drums on my first recording." Eddy gave Bob my number and he flew me to Nashville to record. He also came down and spent almost three weeks with me. It's a hell of a story!

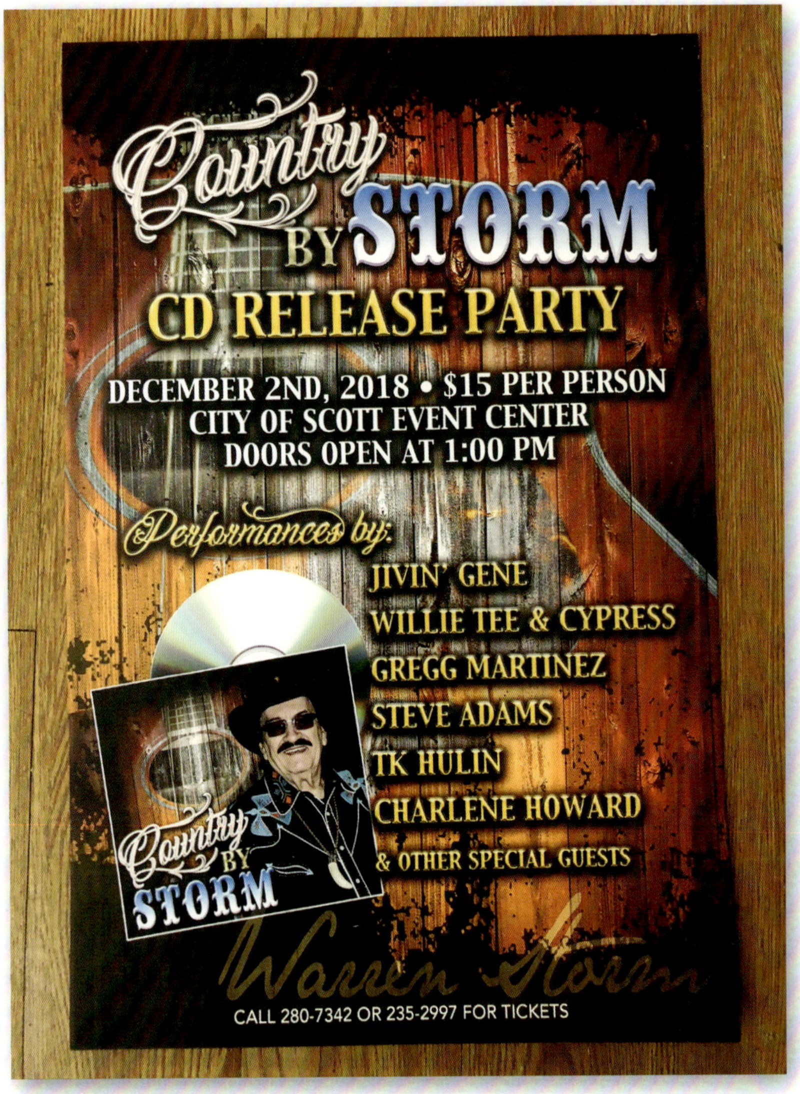

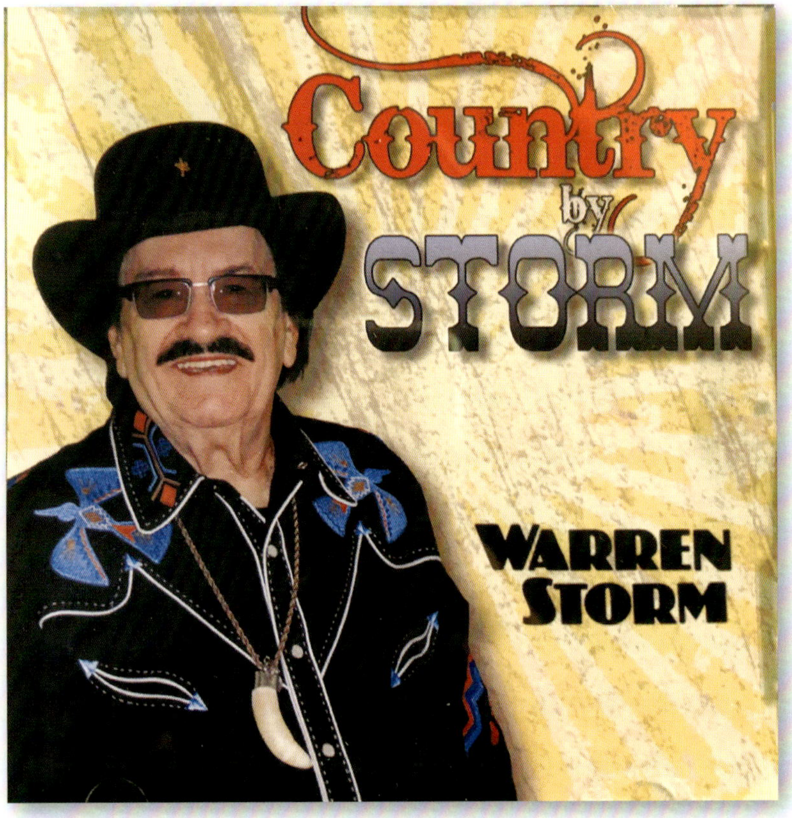

WS: That was like a miracle thing that happened. Bob wasn't even in the music business! That's crazy. And he spent a lot of money to record that album. I think it was something like $30,000!

YL: How did the record do? Did it sell a lot of copies?

WS: I guess it did do well. After it was out, Floyd Soileau leased it from him and put it out on cassette. Then just this past year, it finally got on CD. It was never on a CD before.

YL: Let me get this straight. Floyd, years back, got the masters and released the *Heart and Soul* album on cassette. Then in 2018, he re-released it as *Country by Storm*?

WS: Yes.

YL: Why on earth, some thirty-six years later, Floyd Soileau would even think of the album, much less re-release it?

WS: Well, a musician friend of mine, Milton Guilbeaux, had transferred the album recording to a CD and gave a copy to me and my friend, V.J. "Boulee" Boulet. Boulee started playing it on his radio show, and Floyd heard it and he remembered the songs. Boulee called Floyd and suggested that we put it out again. So, they contacted Bob in Nashville and he gave them the rights to do that, and we decided to give it a different name.

WS: *Country by Storm*. And, we had a great CD release party too.

After knowing Warren for over six decades, I can't describe his personality and talents in this small amount of space and begin to tell it all.

At an early age, I remember Warren sitting behind the drums in these smoked filled bar rooms for countless hours, firing up these half-drunked up crowds. And now, I see him before the multitudes, belting out these songs with crowds in the palms of his hands.

In the early days, he was considered as one of the better drummers in the territory. As a singer, he's considered as a master of his craft. When he sings a song, he "owns" it. He's the only singer I know who can sing a cop out of a speeding ticket!

He is a superb studio musician (singer and drummer). You can tell by the great products he releases every year.

He is never down, always on the up and up, and quick to encourage the younger musicians in any way he can. And Warren always has full compassion for others going through hard times.

That's the Warren I know and he's my kind of people!

—V.J. BOULET

Warren Storm in Printer's Alley, Nashville

YL: Did you do anything in Nashville after the recording?

WS: After that session, I toured everything in Nashville.

YL: Did you sing at the Grand Old Opry while you were there?

WS: No. But, I met Stan Hitchcock. He was walking on the side of the road. He was a country singer and Conway Twitty's road manager.

Warren Storm in Nashville

YL: You have a lot of pictures from that recording session. Was that session more important to you than the other ones? Or did you just take more pictures? What's the story?

WS: Well, the people there took the pictures for me. But that recording was a big step in my musical career.

YL: How so?

WS: It was Nashville. Very few people get the opportunity to record there, especially in the 1980s. I had recorded there before in the 1960s with Boots Randolph and all them, through J.D. Miller. To have the opportunity to do it again…well, that was another exciting thing in my musical life.

WS: That's Johnny Cash's brother's house right next door to Bob Hendricks. That's how we met him. Ain't that something? Roy Cash, he's dead now.

Top left: Warren Storm in front of Roy Cash's house

Middle left: Warren Storm and Roy Cash

Bottom left: Carrie Cloveree (Johnny Cash's mother) with Warren Storm and Jay Jackson (Hendersonville, TN)

Above: Warren Storm at the Johnny Cash Museum (Nashville, TN)

YL: You've mentioned recording at several different studios with a variety of musicians, styles, and labels, but J.D. Miller's name always seems to be in the mix.

WS: I spent fifteen years recording for J.D. Miller before I went with Huey Meaux. I recorded for him in Crowley and Nashville. He also took me to Cosimo Recording Studio in New Orleans. Cosimo was a well-known rhythm and blues studio. Everybody recorded there–Fats Domino, Little Richard, everybody. I did some session work there.

WS: I remember doing a session with Dr. John. He was a staff musician there. That was before he became famous. Did you know his real name was Malcolm John Rebennack? That's Dr. John's real name!

WS: I also recorded at La Louisiane during that time, on Dale & Grace's No. 1 hit, "I'm Leaving It Up to You."

Warren Storm and Dr. John (New Orleans, 2007)

YL: Did you record any of your own songs at La Louisiane?

WS: Well, I was mostly a session drummer and recorded with other people there. Later on, Huey Meaux recorded some of my stuff there. Then I signed a contract to record with Huey Meaux for another fifteen years. That was in Pasadena, Texas, and in Houston. He had two studios.

YL: What was the name of Huey Meaux's studio?

WS: The Sugar Hill Studio. Huey also took me to record at Cosimo Studio and also a studio in Jackson, Mississippi, but I don't remember that studio name. But I did a session for Adco Records while I was in Jackson. I did four sides but only two came out.

YL: I've never heard of Adco Records.

WS: See, that was Atlantic Records. The white artists recorded on Adco Records, like Bobby Darren and me. And the blues artists were on the Atlantic label.

YL: What songs did you record?

WS: "Nobody Would Know," written by Robert Thibodeaux out of St. Martinville, Louisiana. He was a great writer, man. He wrote some songs for T.K. Hulin too. I was fortunate to record one.

WS: The other song was titled "Rock Down in My Shoe."

WS: I also recorded some songs for CBS Records with Huey while I was in Houston recording for him.

WS: And, I recorded for Floyd Soileau when he had his studio in Ville Platte, Louisiana. And don't forget about Paragon Recording Studio in Chicago. I did that blues CD for George Paulus, and I also recorded with a bunch of people that used to record for Sun Records–rockabilly artists, but I can't remember their names right now.

YL: Let's talk about the labels you've recorded on.

WS: I was on five major labels in my recording career. CBS, Adco, NASCO [*pause*] I can't really remember the other two. When I find them, I'll let you know! Right now, I can't think of it.

[*Warren pauses for another second…*]

WS: Oh! I remember the other labels, ABC-Paramount and Dot Records. Pretty cool, huh?

WS: Oh, there's one more label out of London, Kingfish Records. They just re-released my songs that I recorded at the Sugar Hill Studio.

YL: So, you didn't record abroad?

WS: No, I did not.

WS: Let me show you something. I just got the one of these. It's my CD that has forty-four songs on it. It's not open, but I have to show you this.

[*Warren opens CD…*]

WS: The people from Ace Records, they come down here and go to different studios where you've recorded and they lease your songs. They're one of the biggest companies in the UK that reissues records.

WS: They got this from the Huey Meaux vaults. Remember, Huey Meaux had the studio in Houston. Ace Records is something, man. They're out of England. They got all the labels here that I recorded on. *And,* I still got fifty tunes there that has never been released.

YL: Wait…you still have fifty songs that were not released?

WS: Yes.

YL: Who has them?

WS: I don't know whose got the masters. I recorded those songs in Crowley and in Houston. They still on tape, I guess.

YL: Is ACE Records still around?

WS: Yes. They're out of London.

YL: Let's talk about Huey Meaux. How did the two of you meet?

WS: Oh, that was in 1958. We played in Port Arthur, Texas. We used to play on Sundays at the Pleasure Pier, right by the river, and he was the emcee.

YL: Was he a record producer at the time?

WS: No, he was a barber. But he had a radio show, so that's how he got started. He started producing different singers. He really became successful doing that. He produced B.J. Thomas, Barbara Lynn, Freddy Fender, Warren Storm, Tommy McLain, T.K. Hulin, and Jivin' Gene.

WS: He was a good producer, but he turned bad at the end.

YL: What happened?

WS: Life. I'd rather not talk about it. It was terrible. He was arrested and did some penitentiary time.

YL: Let's move on. You've got pictures here from the Nashville Fan Fair? Tell me about that gig.

WS: It was a festival for the fans of a few major recording artists. A fan appreciation party, I guess. I went there and performed with my good friend, Jimmy C. Newman. Look, that's him right there.

WS: Jimmy used to be in charge of the Cajun portion of that thing, but I don't think they have that anymore.

Warren Storm and Jimmy C. Newman (Fan Fair, Nashville, TN, 1984)

Nashville Fan Fair (1984)

Left: Rodney Miller, Walter (unknown last name), Freddy Fender, V.J. Boulet, Warren Storm, George Belote, and Jim Olivier

Harriet Schexnider, Warren Storm, Jim Olivier, CJ Angelle, JoJo Angelle, Gloria and Willie "Tee" Trahan ("Krewe de Foux," Mardi Gras, 1987)

YL: In 1985, you recorded at Sugar Hill Studios in Houston, Texas. What was that for?

WS: That was for a Jim Olivier's record called *La Musique de Jim Olivier*. I recorded on all of his records. Freddy Fender just happened to be in the studio, so he took his picture with us. It was a Cajun music session.

YL: Who are these guys?

WS: Rodney Miller, George "Muscles" Belote, he played bass guitar, Jim Olivier on vocal, Aldus Mouton played accordion, Freddy Fender, V.J. Boulet on piano, and Warren Storm on drums.

YL: Were you and Jim friends prior to recording?

WS: Yes. I'd known and been friends with Jim for a long, long, long time. I met him through Rod Bernard and from Channel 10. They were both radio announcers too.

WS: I played drums on all of Jim's albums. He had four or five recordings. And, I was on his TV show in the mornings and things like that. I'd known him probably twenty years before we went into the recording studio.

WS: This bottom picture was taken at a Mardi Gras party with Jim Olivier. Fun times, man.

YL: Let's get back to Warren Storm and Cypress. In 1992, you recorded *Night after Night*, on Jen Records, with some of the Cypress Band members. Where did you do that?

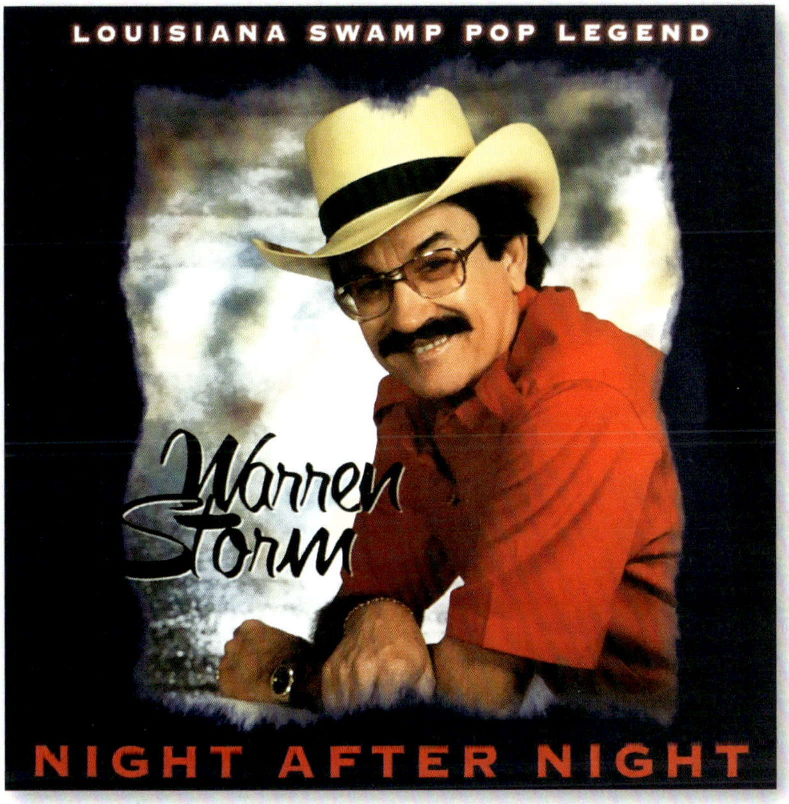

WS: That's right, and we're still together. [*laughing*]

YL: Tell me about some of the places that you've traveled and venues you've played throughout the world.

WS: The first time I traveled abroad was twenty years ago. Me and Johnnie Allan went to England. We did our swamp pop segments and Belton Richard and D. L. Menard did their Cajun part. We all went together and did that show.

WS: We played with musicians from out there. They backed us up. We were playing in London, England. We stayed about four or five days. Oh, and Tommy McLain was on the show too! We were three of us. That was the first time that I flew overseas. That was about twenty or twenty-two years ago. I think I have pictures of that too.

WS: That's me, Tommy McLain, D. L. Menard, and a blues singer from England. I forgot his name. We were in England. Johnnie Allan and Belton Richard where there too.

WS: Three of these guys are gone! Unbelievable.

WS: La Louisiane Studio in Lafayette, Louisiana. Jen Records, but that was really Floyd Soileau. He would just rent the studio and then put it on his label.

YL: What caused Warren Storm, Willie Tee, and Cypress to initially split up?

WS: Willie went play with the Boogie Kings for quite a while, and I just did spot jobs with different groups around the clubs, you know.

YL: You're saying you didn't have another band until the Cypress Band got back together?

Warren Storm, Tommy McLain, D. L. Menard, Jimmy Anderson, Johnnie Allan, and Belton Richard (London, England, September 1993)

WS: They made me shave my mustache so I could look like I was in the 50s. They wanted Tommy to shave his too. He said, "Okay, I'll do it," but he didn't!

YL: These might be the only pictures I've seen of you outside of high school without a mustache!

WS: Yep, could be.

WS: Can you believe that? They made me shave my mustache!

YL: When did you decide to grow and keep your mustache?

WS: I started that in 1974.

YL: Do you remember the venue where these photos were taken?

Warren Storm (The Grand Theatre, Clapham, London, September 18, 1993, Photo by Paul Harris)

WS: The Clapham Theatre in London, England. This is where they did all of the Vaudeville shows. But we did a Cajun show and a swamp pop show. We all flew over there together. I think the theme was "Another Louisiana Saturday Night."

WS: That's my friend, Dave Thomas. He flew in from England, and came to the Back-to-Back Club in Lafayette to hear us live. That was probably a few months after we had played in England. They flew all the way down, just to hear us over here.

YL: Were you nervous to fly overseas?

WS: Not really. Flying doesn't bother me at all.

WS: I went back to England two more times. First, with Lil' Band O' Gold, then I went to England and did another show with musicians from over there. I also went to Holland five times and played different shows there.

Warren Storm (The Grand Theatre, Clapham, London, September 18, 1993, Photo by Paul Harris)

He was a Cat Daddy then and he's a Cat Daddy now! I started recording with Brother Warren in the late '70s and before he was the "Godfather of Swamp Pop" he was a bad mam'a jam'a. A great singer, powerful drummer, and the coolest dude I know. Warren brings the soul every time he opens his mouth, making even his covers his own. He has worked with the legends in South Louisiana and he has joined their ranks and rightfully so. I am so proud to be called his friend and let me just say, "WARRRRRRREN" "SON!"

I love you my brother!

—Freddie Pate

Warren Storm and Dave Thomas

WS: I would just get on the plane by myself and go. I would never do that again!

WS: Of course, I traveled often with Lil' Band O' Gold. We went to Australia and New Zealand three times.

YL: Australia, huh?

WS: Yes. I remember I wanted to see some kangaroos. Those festival people must have drove me eighty miles, just so I could see some kangaroos, man! We came to this place and they were all outside. I was from here to the wall to the kangaroos. They were just hanging around. They had one of them kangaroos in the pouch, I said, "Get out of there, you!" David Egan busted out laughing. He never forgot that.

WS: Aw...we had a lot of fun...but I couldn't do it again. That's a long way. We'd have to drive six hours between gigs. One time, we flew across the continent, five hours, just to get to the next gig. Wow. That's how big that continent is! I'm glad I did it, but I could never do it again. I will not travel anymore...unless they got *A LOT* of money. [*laughing*] And you know, they don't have a lot of money!

WS: We also did a show in Nice, France.

YL: How'd you get to go to France?

WS: The city of Lafayette got us out there to play. It was a big deal.

YL: Did your wife, Harriet, ever travel with you?

WS: My wife never traveled with me. She'd come to local shows, but never overseas.

YL: If you could go back and play anywhere again, where would it be?

Warren Storm (Nice, France, 2009)

"Just like people say what's your favorite song? My answer is always, 'They're all my favorite.'"

WS: Oh, I'm going to tell you right now! It's London, England. They got so much stuff to see. I really love that place. I've been there four or five times, and just love it. There's so much history.

WS: Washington, D.C., that's very historical. I'd go back there too.

YL: Here's a hard question. What was your favorite place to play?

WS: I had so many. Do you mean out of the country or clubs? Well, it doesn't matter. I enjoyed all of them. That's the thing. I can't choose. Just like people say what's your favorite song? My answer is always, "They're all my favorite." And it shows. Because you know every time I perform I enjoy it so much to see the people enjoy the music and dancing. That's what it's all about.

YL: Do you find that the dancing aspect of the music is changing?

WS: Not where we play. Because they're kind of hungry for the old music. I don't think it'll ever die. Old country and the music we do, it's rhythm and blues, swamp pop, whatever you want to call it. People love it because it's dancing music.

YL: What about the younger generation? Do you see them dancing?

WS: No. And that's sad.

YL: You're called "The Godfather of Swamp Pop" because you're the oldest of the musicians playing that style of music. Did you ever think you would be eighty-two years old?

WS: Nope.

YL: What's it like to be eighty-two and still a working musician?

WS: Oh, I don't know. It's like I just live from day to day.

WS: When I was in school, I thought thirty was old! When I was seventeen, I'd say, "Thirty years old, that's old, man!" [*laughing*] The weeks and the months go so fast now.

[*Warren pauses and reminisces...*]

WS: You know what I used to get for Christmas when I was young and lived in Leroy? I'd get a big Mr. Goodbar. That's what I'd get. It was huge! I must have been seven or eight years old, or something like that. That was my gift. Back then the houses were off the ground. We'd play underneath them with wooden blocks. That was our toys. When they would do carpenter work, we'd get them and that was our toys.

YL: Did you ever use the blocks as an instrument? Or was it just a building block.

WS: No. I never used them as drums. I just built things with them. But I used the pots and pans though!

YL: Anything else you want to share before we stop for today?

WS: [*laughing*] Only that I just love this. I never thought anybody would write the history of my life and music.

WS: Oh, I want to show you something before you go.

[*Warren brings out a box full of 45 records...*]

YL: Whoa! Is that all you? It looks like you have every record that you ever recorded.

WS: Almost all of them. I have different record collectors from all over the world that send me my records when they find them. My friend Larry, from Baltimore, is always looking. He sends them to me when he finds them.

WS: Look at my collection. It's unbelievable!

[*Warren takes out each record carefully...*]

WS: These are my four NASCO release records. I have them organized in Ziploc bags by who they were released with. I was on Atlantic Records too! One recording. This one right here. You see friends that are record collectors find my records that are in mint condition. I just want to show you a few of them. This is the first one, the "Prisoner's Song" and "Mama, Mama, Mama." That's the one that started it all. I got quite a few copies of those, but I only did four 45 records on NASCO. Let me see if I can find the other one.

[*Warren keeps looking...*]

WS: I'll find it later on. How you like that?

[*Warren continues looking through his records and then says...*

WS: Maybe later on, when you come back, we can play all these things! We can have a listening party!

[*Warren holding up a 45 record...*]

WS: Did you know I recorded "This Could Go on Forever" first? Before Rod Bernard? His version made the hit though.

YL: How does it make you feel to pull out a huge box of records that are all your recordings? Seems like there's at least one hundred records here with your name on them.

"If you can't have fun, and enjoy yourself on stage while you're performing, then you better stay home."

WS: Well it's unbelievable! You know I'm fortunate to still be here to talk about all that stuff. That's what's amazing! And I can't believe there's going to be a book about it. That's amazing in itself!

YL: Yes, Warren, that *is* pretty amazing. I'm looking at this box, and these are just the 45s! You don't even have the albums that you've recorded on in here. Nor are these the records that you recorded as a studio musician. How many of them did you record on?

WS: Well, I recorded with about eight or ten or twelve blues artists on Excello playing drums. But my records were on NASCO. That was in the 1950s and early 1960s. Now, there's so many that I recorded on, I don't know.

WS: Do you think after we're finished talking, I can play you a few of my records? I have a record player!

YL: You sure can.

YL: I wonder, was there ever a point in your life where you thought maybe you just didn't want to play music anymore?

WS: Never. That's what I was made to do. And you know every time I'm on the stage, it's like brand new. I enjoy making people dance and listen, you know.

WS: I always said, "If you can't have fun, and enjoy yourself on stage while you're performing, then you better stay home." You know what I mean?

[*Warren takes out his old record player that his daughter found for him and proceeds to play some of his records.*]

Warren Storm and Lionel Prevost (Bridge City, TX)

WS: The first record I'm gonna play is the one I did in Birmingham with Johnny Cash, "Troubles on My Mind." I'm playing drums and singing. Katie Webster is on the piano and that's Lionel Prevost, the hired sax player from Port Arthur. This is 1959 now!

WS: Lionel Prevost was a good friend of mine who played on a lot of sessions with me in Crowley. A great sax player... great sax player.

[*Warren continues listening to "Troubles on My Mind"...*]

WS: What do you think about that?! And that one's not in mint condition.

WS: I'll play you one I recorded at Cosimo Studio. Sam Cooke's drummer played on this one. It's called "Take These Chains from My Heart." It's an old Hank Williams song. That's all of Fats Domino's band backing me up! They were a union band. All I had to do was sing.

[*Warren plays the record…*]

WS: That was in 1965, or something like that. Katie Webster played the piano on that recording again.

WS: You heard that drummer? He was on the road with Sam Cooke. They happened to be in town, and the studio called him. I remember he asked me, "How you want me to play that?" I said, "Whatever you do, the way you do it."

WS: So, Fats Domino's band played on this record, except for Katie. She came from Lake Charles and we rode together to record this song. And of course, Sam Cooke's drummer.

[*Warren is still sifting through the stack of 45s…*]

WS: You got time for one more?

YL: Yes, sir.

WS: Man, I haven't heard these songs in ages!

[*Warren sings along. Then asks…*]

WS: One more?

YL: Absolutely, but I have a question. I know, as a person gets older, their voice tends to drop. And when I listen to these songs, your vocal range is pretty high. When you sing these songs today, do you have to lower the keys in order to hit some of those notes?

[*Instead of answering the question, Warren proceeds to sing the song we just heard in the same key as the record.*]

WS: I was a lot younger then. That's why it sounds like that. But I can still hit it.

WS: How you like that?!

YL: What are you going to play now?

WS: How about "Tennessee Blues." My friend Bobby Charles wrote that one. Sonny Landreth recorded on that song with me.

WS: Look at this record, it's in mint condition. We did a remake of "Mama, Mama, Mama" on the other side.

WS: Listen! That's Sonny Landreth playing the guitar right there. I think I did that in the early 1970s.

YL: Who's playing harmonica?

WS: There was a band from Texas that came to record at J. Miller's studio, the Texas Cookin' Band. I asked their harmonica player if he'd play on the song. How you like that?

[*Warren takes out another 45 record…*]

WS: Oh! You're going to like this one. This was my wife's favorite song, "Precious Loving You." Look at it. It's in mint condition.

WS: You know, Wayne Morris wrote that song. He was from around Baton Rouge. He was a singer there.

WS: This is a band from Houston that used to come down and record with me. The Texas Cookin' Band with Freddy Pate, that's who backed me up on that song. Randy Corn is on the guitar.

[*Warren's friend V.J. Boulet comes to visit.*]

[*Knocking loudly…*]

WS: Come in! Come in, you modified socket!

VJB: Warren, you just re-released your original *Heart and Soul* album.

WS: Yes.

VJB: Do you think you'll make some money off of this album?

Warren Storm is a swamp pop treasure. I first met him on April 26, 1979, when he agreed to be interviewed for my book *South to Louisiana: The Music of the Cajun Bayous*, which was eventually published in 1983. The interview was conducted at the Scottish Motel in Lafayette, just off I-10. Is it really forty years ago, when it seemed that swamp pop had seen its best days? That the music is stronger than ever today is due in no small measure to Warren and his fellow pioneers, such as Johnnie Allan, Rod Bernard, Bobby Charles, and Tommy McLain, also the younger generation, including Yvette Landry and The Jukes. The Cajun music revival has helped too.

At the time of our interview, I was familiar with Warren's early recordings for J.D. Miller at his Crowley studio, including the 1958 Top 100 national hit, "Prisoner's Song" (on the Nasco label). I also knew that Warren was Miller's session drummer into the 1960s, and recorded with hallowed swamp bluesmen such as Slim Harpo, Lightnin' Slim, Lazy Lester, and Lonesome Sundown, among many other stylists.

As the interview unfurled–and as this book will tell–more information and color was added to his story. We discussed the impact of his father, Simon Schexnider, a drummer and multi-instrumentalist who played classic Cajun and hillbilly music with the marvelously named Lucky Go Ramblers of Abbeville, Happy Fats and the Rayne-Bo Ramblers, and Lawrence Walker's Wandering Aces. Warren's own musical heroes were Hank Williams, Fats Domino, and Elvis Presley, masters of their craft all, and those inspirational New Orleans drum masters Earl Palmer and Charles "Hungry" Williams.

With this stellar background allied to Warren's considerable talent, it's easy to understand his eventual recognition as the "Godfather of Swamp Pop."

His many recordings for the great J.D. Miller, Paul Cohen with the Nashville "A" team session men, Huey Meaux, Carol Rachou, Floyd Soileau, Mark Miller, and others are historical documents of a uniformly high standard, with Warren's vocals invariably drenched in soul–try his "Seven Letters" for an emotion-wracked experience. As for live music, he has continuously entertained audiences at clubs and festivals throughout South Louisiana and elsewhere with The Wee-Wows, The Jive Masters, The Shondells with Rod Bernard and Skip Stewart, Bad Weather, Willie Tee and Cypress, and Lil' Band O' Band, among others.

"Everywhere he has carried the swamp pop flag with ambassadorial pride, and always with a big smile."

Through the years, I have been privileged to see Warren perform many times in Lafayette, New Orleans, New York, the Netherlands, and my home country of England. Everywhere he has carried the swamp pop flag with ambassadorial pride, and always with a big smile.

I have recently updated *South to Louisiana* in a new second edition–it's about time!–and was delighted to quote Warren on the back cover saying, "Thank you for caring so much about our music." In turn, we should all thank him for all he's done for South Louisiana music–and all he continues to do.

—JOHN BROVEN
AUTHOR OF *SOUTH TO LOUISIANA: THE MUSIC OF THE CAJUN BAYOUS*

WS: Well, the only money you make is when you perform live. But I'm used to not making money! Yep, that's what I said, "I'm used to not making money." What else is new man? [*laughing*]

YL: But you recorded so many songs!

WS: In the old days, the promoter and the record companies kept everything. Songs that I recorded, I never really got paid for that.

YL: You're releasing the old *Heart and Soul* album as a country album, *Country by Storm*. People around here know you as the "Godfather of Swamp Pop." Do they even know that you made a country album?

WS: Oh, I did a lot of country in my day. But, I haven't done a lot of country lately, so this'll be like a new project. Something new for people to listen to.

VJB: Son!

WS: SON!

YL: That seems to be your signature saying. Where did that come from?

WS: Oh, I heard that on the *Porter Wagoner Show*. Jerry Reed said that too! Everybody calls me "SON," but I've been called a lot worse than that! [*laughing*]

YL: Did you ever have anybody fight with you at a bar, or did you see any fights while playing?

WS: Did they fight?! They used to come there *just* to fight! Gangs, man! People used to go to the Midway Club just to fight! They used to have five bouncers at that club. Palombo's Club, getting into Abbeville, we'd call it the "Bloody Bucket!"

WS: And then, some places had chicken wires on the bandstand so that when they'd throw bottles it wouldn't hit the musicians.

WS: Did they fight?! Did they fight?!

WS: Boulee, right here, used to own a bar. It was called Boo Boo's Night Club, on the Breaux Bridge Highway. People would fight all the time. I remember Boulee got two or three deputies to park their cars outside. When the people would fight, the deputies would put them in the car, drive them down the road, and handcuff them to the water tower in Breaux Bridge. Then, every few hours, the deputies would come back around and kick them in the ass. They would get eaten by mosquitoes!

WS: In about two or three months, there were no more fights in his club. The word got out and after that, all he needed was one deputy from that point forward.

YL: Did anyone ever go after you for any reason?

WS: No. I was friends with all them outlaws, man! Palombo used to say...he'd get the mic...he'd say, "Look, I don't want no fighting in my place. I don't want no cussing." He said, "The first one that says s***, the piss is gonna fly!"

WS: Let me tell you, they had gangs from all the different small communities, like Delcambre, Erath, and Abbeville. The gangs would come and they'd fight! Bloody fights! One time, we played in Cameron over there at Sweeney's Club. They had a big canal in front of the place, let me tell you, they'd start the fight in the ditch and finish in the canal.

WS: Another time, we played at The Swinging Doors there in New Iberia. A guy got shot in the parking lot. It was like the wild, Wild West!

"Everybody calls me 'SON,' but I've been called a lot worse than that!"

WS: At the old Pat's, when you'd walk in, the bandstand was right there on the left. I'd put my drum cases between the door and the bandstand. One night, they had a fight, and the bouncer told the guy, he said, "You better get out." But the guy kept advancing, and the bouncer shot him in the stomach! The blood flew all over my damn drum cases. I said, "Who's going to clean that?"

WS: [*laughing*] No, I didn't say that. But the rest of the story is true.

WS: Mr. Pat Huval, the owner, used to break up the fights himself. He was scrappy. He was a good fighter himself.

YL: Sounds like things got pretty rough. Did you think about pursuing other hobbies besides music?

WS: I was on a bowling team for ten years. We'd bowl seven and seven. You know the workers would work seven on and seven off, so we would bowl when they were not working. That was our league name, "7 & 7." So, I'd bowl every other Wednesday.

YL: Who was on the team with you?

WS: Oh, I don't know, different people. I did that when I was working at the city hall. In the late sixties, or something like that.

YL: Were you any good?

WS: My average was 165. That's pretty good. I don't think I could even lift a bowling ball now!

YL: Let's talk about Fats Domino. He pretty much shaped who Warren Storm is today. Did you know him personally?

WS: I knew him for a long time. I remember one time, he came to our sound check in 2007, at Tipitina's in New Orleans. We were doing a Fats Domino Tribute with Robert Plant. Robert Plant also came to the studio and we recorded some Fats Domino songs with Lil' Band O' Gold.

Fats Domino and Warren Storm (1975)

WS: Fats Domino. That's my idol. That picture was in 1975. That was in some little club in the country, by Basile, Louisiana. I forgot the name of the club. But anyway, Fats was playing with some musicians I knew. They took me backstage. That wasn't my first time meeting him, though. I had met him dozens of times before.

WS: The first time I met him I think was on the Breaux Bridge Highway at the Forrest Club. Then, I met him in Cecilia. He played at Shookta's at four corners, a long time ago, child. I've seen Fats about thirty times in my lifetime. I even have a video of him.

YL: Tell me about this Fats Domino tribute with Lil' Band O' Gold and Robert Plant.

Warren Storm and Robert Plant (New Orleans)

WS: We were doing a Fats Domino tribute and Robert Plant, the lead singer of Led Zeppelin, came in and sang some Fats Domino songs with the Lil' Band O' Gold. We backed him up.

WS: Now, me and Robert are friends. They got musicians from all over the world to do the Fats Domino tribute, and he was one of them. He flew to New Orleans to do that with us. I had never met him before that. But, he knew who I was!

YL: How did Robert Plant know who you were?

WS: Because the English people, they all love Louisiana music. He had heard my stuff before. He was a fan. You know who else is a fan? Lily Allen. We played her wedding reception in England. She's a pop star from England. She's friends with Prince Charles's wife. It was the Lil' Band O' Gold that played that.

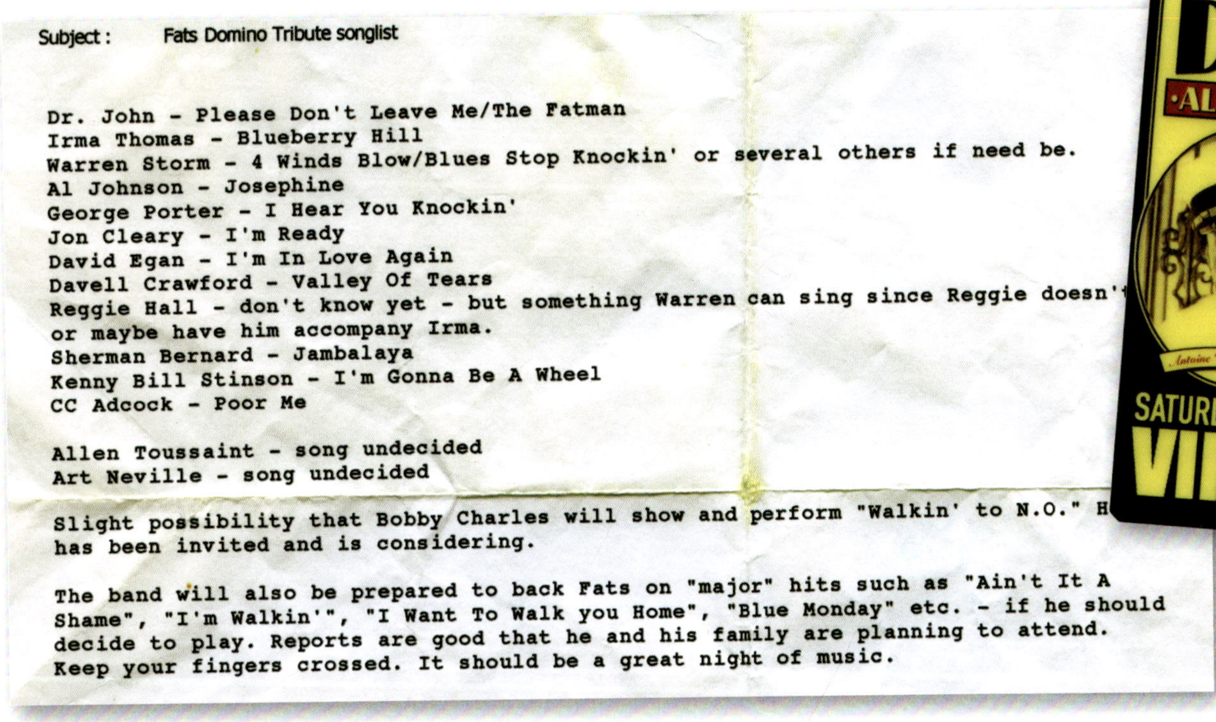

Subject : Fats Domino Tribute songlist

Dr. John - Please Don't Leave Me/The Fatman
Irma Thomas - Blueberry Hill
Warren Storm - 4 Winds Blow/Blues Stop Knockin' or several others if need be.
Al Johnson - Josephine
George Porter - I Hear You Knockin'
Jon Cleary - I'm Ready
David Egan - I'm In Love Again
Davell Crawford - Valley Of Tears
Reggie Hall - don't know yet - but something Warren can sing since Reggie doesn'
or maybe have him accompany Irma.
Sherman Bernard - Jambalaya
Kenny Bill Stinson - I'm Gonna Be A Wheel
CC Adcock - Poor Me

Allen Toussaint - song undecided
Art Neville - song undecided

Slight possibility that Bobby Charles will show and perform "Walkin' to N.O." H
has been invited and is considering.

The band will also be prepared to back Fats on "major" hits such as "Ain't It A Shame", "I'm Walkin'", "I Want To Walk you Home", "Blue Monday" etc. - if he should decide to play. Reports are good that he and his family are planning to attend. Keep your fingers crossed. It should be a great night of music.

List of performers and songs on Fats Domino Tribute record (2007)

YL: How does it make you feel when Robert Plant walks into the studio and he's bowing down to Warren Storm?

WS: Well, he walked into the studio and said, "Do you think I'll be able to take a picture with Warren?" I said, "Yeah, come on. I want to take a picture with you! What you talkin' about."

YL: You were the bigger star in Robert Plant's eyes?

WS: Well yeah, because he was a fan of our music. He even came to my house and picked me up in a limousine!

WS: That's my VIP pass from when we had the album release party for Fats Domino in 2007. That was the last time I saw him. It was the last time we performed, also. See I'm the only one from down here that's on that album. Me and David Egan. He's gone too.

WS: Fats…he was my idol!

WS: That's me, Dr. John and Fats Domino at the House of Blues, in New Orleans.

WS: That's Fats Domino's sax player, I don't know his name. C.C. Adcock, Derek Huston, myself, and another sax player, I don't know his name. Dicky Landry, Herb Hardesty, and that's Miss Ellis, she used to take care of Fats Domino. This must have been for the Fats Domino tribute at the House of Blues in New Orleans. That's five saxophone players right there! Whew!

Fats Domino, Warren Storm, and Dr. John (2007)

Interview continues at Ton's Restaurant in Broussard, Louisiana. Friends and fellow musicians Roddie Romero, Derek Huston, V.J. Boulet, and Luke Bourque join us. Warren walks through the door and is immediately surrounded and greeted by people wanting to say hello, shake his hand, and snap a photograph with him.

YL: Warren, everyone knows you!

WS: When you live long enough, everybody gets to know you!

RR: Hello, Mr. Storm. How's the music going?

WS: There's nothing like music, bruh. It makes you live longer. If it wouldn't have been for music, I'd be long gone.

WS: And having good musician friends, well, it's like having another family.

RR: I get it. When you speak another language that other people don't quite understand, like music, the musicians can all relate.

WS: Lord, those non-musician people, they'll never understand us! [*laughing*]

[*Derek Huston enters…*]

WS: Hey Derek! Good to see you!

DH: Good to see you too! How's the gumbo?

WS: It's good, man! Have a seat.

DH: I heard you got a new CD out.

WS: Yes. I did a session in Nashville in 1983. It was released as an album, but never on a CD, so Floyd Soileau put it on a CD. It was originally called *Heart and Soul*, but now it's called *Country by Storm*. I got "I Need Somebody Bad," "Seven Letters," "Love Me Sherry," "Valley of Tears"…

DH: You made those into country songs?

WS: Yeah. It was Nashville pickers. We let them do whatever they wanted. It was like middle of the road kind of thing. Bob Hendricks from Nashville, the one that produced the LP, he drove down from Nashville to come to the CD Release Party. He's seventy-seven now.

Yvette Landry, Luke Bourque, Warren Storm, Roddie Romero, and V.J. Boulet (Ton's Restaurant, December 2018)

DH: You still sing like you're twenty-five. I've often wondered, how do you keep your voice up?

WS: I don't know. [*laughing*]

DH: You live clean though, right?

WS: Absolutely. Also, every morning, I drink some honey, local honey. You know the opera singers do that too!

WS: Did you know, I can sing *opera...après toi*! [*laughs*]

RR: Last night, we were rehearsing Slim Harpo's "King Bee," and we were wondering if you played on that song.

WS: Absolutely. I played on "Scratch Your Back" too.

DH: How do you remember what sessions you did? You've done so many.

WS: I remember the artists. I played on Slim Harpo, Lazy Lester, Lightning Slim… Katy Webster played piano on my sessions, I played drums on hers, Lonesome Sundown from Baton Rouge. That was all in Crowley. Lightning Slim, he had to wait until his song was released to remember the words to be able to do the song again! He would just make them up in the studio! Them old blues singers, they'd just sing whatever they thought about. They'd just write it on the spot.

[*Warren turns to Roddie…*]

"There's nothing like music, bruh. It makes you live longer. If it wouldn't have been for music, I'd be long gone."

WS: You know me and Derek did some shows in New Orleans with Lil' Band O' Gold.

DH: I remember one show in particular at Tipitina's club in New Orleans. Rufus Thomas had just passed away, so I made an announcement from the stage that this officially made Warren the world's oldest teenager.

WS: Derek, what's that story about that genius in New Orleans...what's his name?

DH: Alan Toussiant. At the time, Alex Rowles was the editor of *Offbeat Magazine*, and he called me up to say they were doing an award show that would honor Fats Domino. He asked me to put together a band for the tribute show. And I said, "That's easy, 'cause that band already exists. You've got to get Lil' Band O' Gold. All those guys just love that music so much and know it so deeply. That's the best thing you could possibly do." So, we had a rehearsal before the show and everyone was there. Art Neville, Dr. John, Walter "Wolfman" Washington, and Alan Toussiant. At rehearsal, there were several people slotted to sing, and I don't remember what song it was, but basically, all those guest artists were standing on the side, in the queue, waiting for their turn to rehearse. Alan was standing on the side of the stage in a suit, looking super dapper and very reserved. Warren was on drums, and after the song was over, I've never seen Alan do this, but he walked across the stage, stepped up on the drum rise, reached over the drums, grabbed Warren's hand, and said, "I haven't heard anyone play the drums like that in a loooong time."

WS: Can you believe that?! That genius! He wrote two or three hundred hits! And he came and shook *my* hand.

DH: I get chicken skin just thinking about it! Coming from him, that means the world, huh?

WS: Yes. Yes, it does.

Warren Storm and Fats Domino (New Orleans, LA, 2007)

Pat Breaux, Fats Domino, and Warren Storm (New Orleans, LA, 2007)

DH: I also remember the session when they did the Fats tribute record and we were recording behind Robert Plant–backing him up. As soon as Robert Plant walks in the room, just real cordial, down to earth, Warren walked right up to him and said, "Hey Fred Zeplin, let me get a picture with you."

WS: [*laughing*]

DH: C.C. Adcock said, "Relax Warren, we're gonna be here all weekend." And Warren said, "I may die at any second!" [*laughing*]

WS: I said, "Take the picture, man." That was in 2007.

WS: I also have a video with Fats. He came to our soundcheck and sang. He was outside drinking his Heineken and he said, "Can I sing a song?" I said, "Yes, come on in. We're just setting up." He ended up singing five or six songs. We put the mic on the floor and he sang from the bottom of the stage. At our soundcheck...can you believe that?!

WS: Later, Fats came to the studio, and we was all in the studio. I was sitting on the couch besides Robert Plant...me, Robert Plant, and Fats.

DH: Everyone was excited to meet Fats, including Robert Plant. Fats had no idea who Robert Plant was.

WS: No! No idea. Fats said, "Y'all all look alike!"

DH: Fats walked in the room and Warren said, "Fats Domino! You my idol, bruh."

WS: Fats said, [*singing*] "Ain't that a shame…wish I could say the same!" [*laughing*] Everything you'd tell him, he had an answer for.

WS: What a week that was...whew! You know Robert Plant rented a car and came to my apartment? We rode together. He wanted to see where I recorded, so we went to Crowley together. When I got over there, to the studio, them people over there, they almost fell down. I went to the mayor's office and said, "This is Robert Plant." He said, "WHAT?!"

Fats Domino sax player, Fats Domino, Warren Storm, and Kenny Bill Stenston (New Orleans, LA, 2007)

Warren Storm, Harriet Schexnider, Robert Plant, Heather Daigle, and Julie Daigle (Warren's Apartment, Broussard, LA)

Robert Plant and Warren Storm (New Orleans, LA, 2007)

WS: He called the news media and everything. That was a great day. When he came to my apartment in 2007, my wife was still living, and when I opened the door, he knelt down and kissed Harriet's hand. Lord, she almost passed out, man!

RR: How did y'all record in the early days? Full band? Tracking?

WS: You had to recall that everybody in the band...you couldn't overdub or nothing like that. It was a two-track man. So that's why we spent all night to do one song.

WS: I remember when Clifton Chenier would record to two-track. He didn't take all night. Clifton would say, "That's good enough. I ain't doing that no more." [*laughing*] But it *was* good enough.

WS: I played on some of his recordings. I did the thing he did with Rod Bernard, *Boogie in Black and White*. I played drums on that. We did that at Floyd's in Ville Platte.

RR: Y'all used to cut up in those days?

WS: [*laughing*] Absolutely.

YL: I can't get Warren to tell me any of *those* stories!

WS: Well, you know...I told you the good things! [*laughing*]

DH: I've got another question for you...What's up with the gloves when you play?

WS: That's so I could hold my sticks, so they wouldn't slip. Better grip.

DH: When did you start that?

WS: When I was playing with Lil' Band O' Gold. I was playing so hard because C.C. Adcock was so damn loud! He had three amplifiers. [*laughing*] On top of that, I'd have to play with the big end of the sticks just so I could hear myself. Roddie knows...he played with us sometimes.

My relationship with Warren Storm goes back some fifty-five years of music. We are very close friends, more like family. I can honestly say it has been a beautiful ride all these years. Warren possesses many special attributes. He has never let his popularity go to his head. He treats all the musicians with great respect and in turn, all musicians treat him likewise. He never criticizes or belittles any musician no matter how inexperienced they may be. He never skips over a musician to take a "ride" when he is performing. He takes great pride in all his performances, always giving his very best! Warren has truly been a brother to me throughout our music lives. He has soul and can sing just about any song and make it sound as if he wrote it. He has been a great inspiration to many young and very experienced musicians throughout his seventy years of performing. His popularity with his swamp pop fans is second to none. They love this performer both singing and playing drums. I have been very fortunate and blessed to have had the relationship I have experienced as a swamp pop musicians and very close friend with Warren Storm.

—Gene R. Romero

WS: Roddie came with us when we played for the Walton's, the family that owns Wal-Mart. They flew us to Arkansas and put us up and everything. Derek and Roddie were both honorary members of the band. Derek would jump in with the horn section.

WS: I asked Robert Plant one time if he ever had horns in his band. He said, "No. We smoked too much dope. We couldn't afford the horns!" [*laughing*] He was funny man. Robert is a good dude.

RR: Do you remember the Bobby Charles Tribute at the House of Blues in New Orleans?

WS: Yeah. Eric, Dr. John, Elvis Costello, they were all there. Elvis Costello, man, that's a very nice guy. He was leaning against the wall and he said, "I can't believe I'm getting a chance to hear Warren Storm play drums." Do you believe that? WOW! Dr. John was there too.

WS: I got an "X-Rated" thing that Dr. John said. All the musicians were in the back room, and I said, "Mac, look! Elvis Costello is walking through the door." Dr. John said, "Good, I didn't like that other son of a bitch anyhow" (i.e. Elvis Presley). Last time I saw Dr. John was when we played a festival in Australia. Dr. John, and Buddy Guy was there too.

DH: One last question, what drummers do you admire?

WS: All of them, if they play well. Buddy Rich...Gene Krupa, he was my first idol in the 1950s.

YL: Did you pattern yourself, style-wise, after anyone or did you just come up with your own style?

WS: I did...Charlie Williams that played with Fats, and Earl Palmer, the greatest R&B drummer ever. He recorded five years at Cosimo before he went to the West Coast. He recorded with everybody. But he started in the ghetto. Earl Palmer—I'm glad I got to meet him a year before he died, at the Ponderosa Stomp. I went on stage and watched him—awesome. He still had it. I loved his sessions with Little Richard..."The Girl Can't Help It"...man.

WS: Bobby Charles told me he went to one of them sessions with Little Richard. He saw him record. He said as the song faded out, the band was supposed to stop, but the band kept playing. They were still jamming twenty minutes after the song finished! Boy, I'd have liked to have heard that man. That's some bad dudes. They were way ahead of their time.

[*Warren starts singing...*]

WS: What a day we're having, man. This makes my day. It beats sitting and watching TV and talking to myself.

[*Warren's phone rings...he says, "Let me see, that might be the President." "Hello."* [*pause*] *"Son!"* [*pause*] *"Who dat?"*]

Caden, Riley Ann, and Erica (2018)

Storm Family Album

YL: We've talked extensively about your music career. Let's talk about family. When did you get married?

WS: I got married in 1960 to Harriet Ann Waguespack. She was born in Erath but she was living with her mama and two sisters in Lafayette. They moved to Lafayette when she was nine years old. She lost her daddy in a wreck that year.

YL: You were the famous "Warren Storm." How did this little Cajun girl catch your eye?

WS: Well, I guess she fell in love, and so did I! We met at her mama's place; she had a lounge. And Harriet came to the dances where I played, all around Acadiana.

YL: I'm sure there were a lot of women who were out at the dances.

WS: Yeah, you're right! But, she was the one. She was sixteen and I was twenty-three when we got married.

WS: We had three children, Donna Lisa, Warren Todd, and Julie Ann Schexnider.

WS: Our first child was Donna Lisa Schexnider, born 1961, my son Todd was born in 1963, and Julie Ann in 1964!

WS: Donna Lisa Schexnider Thibodeaux lives in Picayune, Mississippi, with her husband, Ralph Thibodeaux. She's got one son, Dustin. He plays the guitar...no, my son plays the guitar. My son lives in Marietta, Ohio, with his wife Shelly. He's got three children, one son, Zachery Schexnider, plays the drums like his grandpa. Leila and Erica Schexnider are his daughters.

WS: I have great-grandkids too, Caden and Riley Ann. They belong to Erica. I'll have another great-granddaughter in December. Dustin and his wife are expecting.

Rylin Renae Thibodeaux (Great-granddaughter, 2018)

WS: My daughter, Julie Ann Schexnider Daigle, lives in Broussard with her husband Tommy Daigle. She's the only one living close by…her and my granddaughter, Heather Daigle, soon-to-be Melancon. She's getting married in September 2018. She comes have lunch with her Paw-Paw every day. And she's tall!

Heather Daigle and Warren Storm

WS: I got five grandchildren and three great grandchildren.

YL: Where did you get married?

WS: Harriet and I got married at St. John's Cathedral in Lafayette, in 1960. It was a small wedding, maybe twenty friends. We went to New Orleans on our honeymoon. We got to see live music. Sam Butera and The Witnesses were playing, and that's all I wanted to see was them. Sam had played music forever. He was a great sax player and always had a great band. Then we went to the beach and everything.

YL: Did Harriet work or was she busy raising children?

WS: Harriet was a house wife and at one time we both worked for the city of Lafayette. She was a key puncher and I was in the printing department. They called it the duplicating department back then.

YL: How long did you do that for?

WS: I did that for fifteen years and she did it for about eight or nine years. But I played music the whole time. I'd work from 8–5 p.m., then I'd play on Mondays and Tuesdays in Lake Charles then go back to work at 8:00 a.m. the next morning.

YL: Where'd you play in Lake Charles?

WS: I'd play at Phil's Gusher on Broad Street. It was during the oil boom. It was just three of us. Me, Everette Brady (bass), and Glen Guidry on the piano. Piano, bass, and drums; and all three of us sang. I don't have a picture of that band. I wish I did.

YL: Do any of your children play music?

WS: My son, Todd. He's got about fifteen guitars and my grandson Zach, he plays drums in Ohio.

YL: What do your kids think about your musical career?

WS: They all love music. Zach and Todd have a little rock group over there in Ohio. But they don't have our kind of music.

WS: I told them, "Y'all need to come over here! We got so much music here." They want to come so bad.

WS: I told Zach, "You better learn your Paw-Paw's songs, baw!"

WS: I don't know if he will. He's got a double bass drum and the whole works! He sent me a recording of him playing drums. He's into that heavy metal stuff. I told him, "I can see what you doing, you playing the hell out of them drums! But that dang music! Rhar, rhar, rhar, oh man."

WS: I told my grandson, "Play either Cajun, swamp pop, or country music. You're going to make money playing those three things."

YL: Do they visit often?

"I'm really fortunate that God let me live this long, you know what I mean?"

Above: Zach Schexnider (Warren's grandson)

Left: Zach Schexnider (drums), Warren Storm (bass), Todd Schexnider (guitar), Ralph Thibodeaux, and Harriet Schexnider

Left: Julie Ann Schexnider, Middle and right: Warren at home on Sage Glenn

WS: No. It's too hard. He's got three children and two grandchildren, so it's too expensive for everyone to travel. And I can't afford to go.

WS: But I did go see them a couple of times, me and my wife, through the years. We'd fly out there. One time I had a friend who took us out there in a motorhome. It's a twenty-hour drive.

YL: Do you have time for a few more questions?

WS: Oh yeah. I'm in no hurry. Like my grandson Dustin said when he was seven years old, "I'z ain't goin' nowherez."

WS: He's twenty now.

YL: Being a full-time musician is challenging to say the least. And the difficulty of being married to a full-time musician is probably multiplied exponentially. Temptations abound.

YL: You and Harriet were married for fifty-two years. How did you and your marriage survive drugs, alcohol, groupies, and other temptations that have derailed many music careers?

WS: Well, I wasn't perfect. I didn't do hard drugs, but, I did take some pills to stay awake through the years. I drank too, but very little. The pills were to help me stay awake when I drove back to Abbeville from late night gigs.

WS: I guess I must have stopped everything at the right time. If you keep on doing stuff like that, it'll ruin you.

YL: Did you have friends that "didn't stop at the right time"?

WS: Yes, and they're all dead. I had musician friends that played with me, and they never did stop. Smoking and drinking and taking drugs…that's not good.

YL: Did Harriet make you quit?

WS: Nope. She never said anything about that. But, I didn't abuse anything, you know. Thank God, I had some self-discipline.

WS: I'm really fortunate that God let me live this long, you know what I mean?

YL: He's got bigger plans for you Warren Storm.

WS: [*laughing*] Thank you Jesus.

YL: What about women? I'm sure there were lots of temptations through the years.

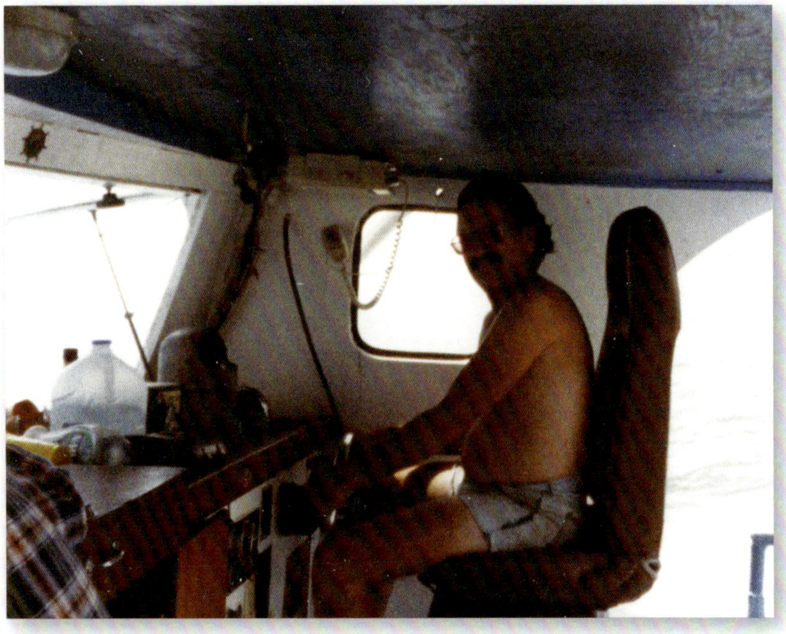

Vermilion Bay (1982)

WS: Again, I wasn't perfect. We/I had some rough times in my marriage. But thanks to Harriet, she guided me along and straightened me up. Fifty-two years we lived together.

YL: That says a lot about Harriet's character.

WS: You talk about! You better believe it. A strong woman saves a man.

WS: I recorded a song in Nashville one time that always reminded me of her, "I Can't Be Me Without You."

YL: As busy as you were playing music, you found time to go fishing with your wife?

WS: Yes, in Vermilion Bay. We caught 700 pounds of shrimp and about 70 dozen crabs. Mr. Chester Smith had a big, big, big, big boat. I drove that big boat–talk about something.

WS: This was one time when in snowed in 1988.

YL: How long has Harriet been gone?

WS: It'll be seven years in September. September 20.

Warren Storm, Julie Schexnider Daigle, Harriet Schexnider, Donna Schexnider Thibodeaux, and Todd Schexnider

Schexnider Family (Dustin and Chantelle's Wedding, New Orleans, LA)

YL: If I may ask, what happened?

WS: She had a tumor on her liver. Four months from the diagnosis, she was gone.

YL: Wow. That was really fast.

WS: Well, she had been sick for years. She'd throw up all the time. Harriet thought she was just allergic to dairy products. Finally, I told her we needed to go to the doctor. We waited too long. The doctor said the tumor was the size of a volleyball. Hard-headed, I guess, not wanting to go to the doctor. Now, I go every six months to get a check-up.

YL: Did music help you get through the grief of losing your wife of fifty-two years?

WS: No, it didn't. Because singing all those old songs we grew up on…that was very, very hard to do. I stayed two weeks without playing, but then I had to play. That was my living. It's still hard to this day. There are a lot of songs I still break up on. It was rough, man. I finally got through it, but I still struggle with losing her. We were together fifty-two years, man.

Schexnider Family (New Orleans, LA, 2004)

[*Warren pauses and wipes tears from his eyes…*]

YL: What else would you like to share about your family?

WS: Just that they are really happy about this project.

Celebrities

In 1948, when Warren was a mere eleven years old, he shook the hand of Hank Williams, who was traveling through Louisiana on the Hadacol Caravan. Hank Williams is considered by many as one of the most significant and influential American singers and songwriters of the 20th century. This simple hand-shake had a profound effect on a young, budding musician. Coming from a poor family, however, Warren had no camera to record this once-in-a-lifetime moment.

Fast forward ten years later to 1958, when Warren's first single hit the national Billboard Chart, just weeks after being released. This hit single got Warren invited to Graceland to sit and visit with Elvis Presley. Again, Warren had no camera to capture the moment.

It was at that moment, Warren knew, he would not miss an opportunity again. He purchased his first camera and proceeded to capture every subsequent important encounter in his musical career. He's still doing it today.

It would take years to go through the innumerable photos that Warren has amassed throughout his career. Of the vast trove of photos that Warren keeps stacked in containers padding every closet in his home, what follows is just a small cross-section.

Dear Warren,
W.T.F? I hear you are coming out with a book. You know I deserve the accolade much more than you. I'm the best that's ever been. I want to wish me the best. I deserve it all.

That being said, I suppose I'd better tell the truth. I can't think of a more deserving person. After all we have been through, you were the one with talent and you are pretty.

Hugs, kisses, and love.
Your soul brother,

—Bobby Page

YL: Let's take a look at some of the celebrities that you've met and played with throughout the years.

YL: I see you've got a picture with the Wilburn Brothers. They were one of country music's great sibling duos. They had thirty chart hits throughout the 1930s-1950s. How'd you meet them?

Wilburn Brothers (1975)

WS: Oh, they came through and did a local thing. I believe it was somewhere by Crowley, Louisiana. They got different musicians to play. Pee Wee Whitewing played, I played drums. It was just a local booking.

YL: Is this Boxcar Willie?

WS: Yes! This was at the Alex Broussard Ranch. All those Grand Old Opry stars used to come and play there.

YL: Did you play with him?

WS: No, we played before him. Look...he even signed the picture for me.

WS: I saw him again in Nashville in 1984.

Warren Storm and Boxcar Willie
(Alex Broussard Ranch, St. Martinville, LA)

Boxcar Willie in Nashville (1984)

Warren Storm and Leroy Van Dyke (1984)

WS: Remember this guy? Leroy Van Dyke, he's a famous recording artist. He had hits with "Auctioneer" and "Walk on By." I met him in Nashville.

John Fogerty, Rockin' Sidney, Mark Miller, Warren Storm, Kippy Bacquet, and Willie "Tee" Trahan (John Fogerty & The All Stars, 1985)

YL: What club did you play?

WS: The Bon Temps Club, on University. Me and Willie were playing six nights a week there. We did that for three years, six nights a week. See, I was a little bit younger than I am now. [*laughing*]

YL: Did they enjoy the music?

WS: They loved what we did.

YL: This looks interesting. What's happening here?

WS: John Fogerty & The All Stars. John came down and re-recorded Rockin' Sidney's song, "My Toot Toot," for Warner Brothers, at J. Miller Studio in Crowley. We also filmed a video of that. I was part of the video. I played drums. It played on Showtime or HBO and was shown all over the world. John's been a huge Louisiana regional roots fan for a long time.

WS: Rockin' Sidney was there with his accordion, and me and Willie Tee all recorded on that. And then, we went out in the country and they had a crawfish boil and everything. They had never ate crawfish before. They documented all that. It's on YouTube, John Fogerty and Friends.

https://youtu.be/uQgHv0cd9E8

WS: Later, that night, I was playing on North University and all the Warner Brothers crew and everybody came.

John Fogerty and Warren Storm (1985)

YL: This poster of Super Pickers, what's that about?

WS: Well, I just got this for a souvenir, but I did play with Buddy Emmons and Phil Baugh for a guitar clinic. I played drums with them when they came to Pangay's near New Iberia.

WS: Now this is pretty awesome. This was at Pangay's in Cade, Louisiana. Harold Romero owned Romero's Music Company and he booked these great musicians from Nashville–Buddy Emmons and Phil Baugh. It was a pedal steel guitar clinic. So, the crowd was basically all musicians. Richard Comeaux (local pedal steel ace) was in the audience that night. He couldn't have been but eighteen or nineteen years old. This was in 1982. Harold brought me a new set of drums and hired me to play with them. Buddy and Phil had sent me a demo to get an idea of what they were going to play. I have a copy that was recorded on a two-track from that night. My friend, and pedal steel player, Milton Guilbeau, has a copy of that night.

WS: Buddy Emmons and Phil Baugh–the two greatest pickers in Nashville. Now, they're all gone.

Phil Baugh, Warren Storm, and Buddy Emmons
(Pangay's Club, Cade, LA)

I recently received a phone call from my friend V. J. Boulet to write some notes about Warren Storm. I was riding down the highway with Wayne Toups when I received the call, on our way to a show in Texas. I thought, how ironic, for I might not be in this vehicle with Wayne, another legend, if not for Warren Storm.

I first met Warren in the mid-80s, I was a teenager. Through the years, he had become friends with my grandparents, Mr. and Mrs. Mitchell Mire. Each year, they would hire Warren and his band to play for their big annual wedding anniversary party in New Iberia. I was still learning how to play music, as a novice, with some of my high school friends at that time. I listened carefully to the big, professional sound that was coming off the bandstand with Warren playing drums and singing along with the band. They sounded incredible! Even then, I picked up on the tone of Warren's voice, full, rich, and pleasing and his one-of-a-kind showmanship. I was familiar with some of the tunes because my grandmother played those Warren Storm albums continuously. One year, probably at the prodding of my grandfather, Warren asked me to sit in with the band. I nervously walked up on the stage, played my few humble guitar licks, and when I was done, Warren and all the band members applauded my efforts. That little bit of encouragement was enough to set in motion what I was going to do with the rest of my life. I wanted to be a music super hero like Warren.

As I slowly came up in the music ranks, we would run into each other, talk about my grandparents, our families, and music. We went on a lot of fishing trips together in Lake Dautrive, Atchafalaya Basin, and some private ponds. Every time I was around his home, I'd stop by and visit. His wife, Mrs. Harriet, always had some delicious food–crawfish pies, cakes, rice and gravy. There was always something comforting about these visits, and we still do it today. There is a genuine love and respect for each other, my superhero, Warren Storm.

In the mid-90s, the group I was in at the time, River Road, had some national success; he was so proud of us, as he knew the other guys in the band as well. Around 1996, I was writing songs, hoping to write a hit for River Road, when I started writing a swamp pop song called "Favorite Dress." It came from my wife at the time, who didn't know what to wear one night. I said, "Put on your favorite dress," and that was it. I wrote it the next day in about ten minutes. As soon as I set the pen down, I immediately called Warren and told him about the song. We went into La Louisiane Studio in Lafayette and recorded "Favorite Dress" and ten other songs for an album project that year, with the River Road guys playing on the tracks. The song was a hit; I was so happy for him. We would go on to write more songs, make more records, and do more shows together as the 1990s came to a close.

Warren Storm has touched so many lives, and has inspired not only me, but countless musicians and entertainers throughout his many decades of performing. Robert Plant from Led Zeppelin traveled all the way from England just to meet him! The word "legend" certainly applies to this man, and the world is a better place because the godfather of swamp pop music rules down here in the swamps of Louisiana!

Thank you, Warren Storm, for sharing your talent and your heart with us all.

Love you, Sonnnnnnnn!

—Steve Grisaffe

Warren Storm, Jerry Springer,
Kenny Bill, and C.C. Adcock (Chicago, IL)

YL: Looking at this picture, I have to ask, were you on the *Jerry Springer Show*?

WS: No, well yes. [*laughing*] We played a gig in Chicago and some guy who owned a bar gave us tickets to the show, so we went as spectators. Talk about crazy! Those people... it's entertainment, I guess.

Doug Kershaw, Mickey Jones, and Warren Storm
(Los Angeles, CA)

Warren Storm and Jerry Lee Lewis
(Grant Street Dancehall, 2006)

WS: That right there is Jerry Lee Lewis. It took me forty years to meet Jerry Lee Lewis. This was at Grant Street Dancehall in Lafayette. All I did was just tell him who I was, shook hands, then he was gone. That's it.

YL: Why do you think it took you so long?

WS: I don't know. We even opened up his show. But, he didn't want nobody backstage at that time.

WS: I tried to take a picture with Jerry Lee Lewis for at least ten years, and I never could do it. Then that night, at Grant Street, his manager said, "Stay right there. He's going to pass and I'll stop him." I had the photographer ready, he shook my hand, snapped the picture, and that was it. Gone. I believe he was having health issues. I think he had a heart attack that night. They were flying out right after the show.

WS: Now this was in 1958. We played a gig in a hotel in Alexandria, Louisiana. We backed up Tex for two nights with my band, the Jive Masters.

YL: How did that come about?

WS: Well, the Jive Masters were booked there and Tex was booked as well. He didn't want to bring a band, so he just asked if we would back him up, you know. That was a good deal!

Tex Ridder (1958)

Warren Storm and Merle Haggard

YL: I can't believe you've actually met all of these people! Merle Haggard? Seriously?

WS: [*laughing*] Yes. Abe Manuel, who is a great local musician, played with Merle Haggard. He's the one that got me to go on the bus and meet him. Merle gave me his book titled *The House of Memories*. Later, I thought it would be great if I gave Merle my 45 record, "My House of Memories." You see, I'm the only one that had a 45 record of that song. So, I brought it to him.

WS: He said, "How you want me to play that?" I said, "You going to have to get you a record player!"

WS: He's a good dude, man. I still have his book, *and* he signed it!

YL: It's amazing that you know all of these people!

WS: I got the good connections. [*laughing*] You got to know somebody that knows somebody. [*laughing*]

Warren Storm and Marty Haggard

Billy Gibbons (ZZ TOP), Warren Storm, and the drummer who played with Stevie Ray Vaughn (Photo by Terri Fensel, 2001)

WS: That's one of Merle Haggard's sons, Marty Haggard. I met him the same time that I met Merle in Baton Rouge.

YL: Who is the gentleman all the way to the right?

WS: That was a drummer who played with Stevie Ray Vaughn. I can't remember his name, but after he heard me play, he gave me his coffin case that he kept his drum sticks in.

YL: Wow. How did meeting these guys come about?

WS: [*laughing*] We played in Houston, Texas, at the Continental Club and at the Continental Club in Austin, with the Lil' Band O' Gold. I met him both times. Billy Gibbons, you know what he said? He said, "My mama is a fan of Warren Storm. She has all of your old records." Can you believe that?!

YL: Was Billy Gibbons performing at the club?

WS: No. He came to watch *me*!

YL: What else did you talk about?

WS: He said, "Mama told me that if I didn't shake your hand, she was going to be mad at me!" So, he shook my hand. I couldn't believe it!

WS: I took this with my good friend, Percy Sledge at Pod-nuh's Nightclub in St. Martinville, Louisiana. We'd back him up with our Cypress Band at different places. He also sang with us when he was inducted into the first Louisiana Hall of Fame. So, I've been knowing him quite a while. Good dude.

WS: Now this was Ray Price. He did a concert at the Municipal Auditorium in Lafayette. We went backstage to watch and meet him and his band. I wasn't playing that night, but I did have a backstage pass.

WS: Another time, when my wife was living, we went to see Ray Price at the old Pangay's. He said, "I want to do a brand-

Warren Storm and Percy Sledge

Ray Price and Warren Storm

new song that's going to be out next week. It's called "For the Good Times." I heard him do it before it was released. I had some goosebumps all over. Wow!

WS: A lot of good memories.

YL: He looks pretty formal in this picture. How was he in person?

WS: Aw, he was awesome, man.

YL: What does one talk about with Ray Price?

WS: Rufus Thibodeaux! Everybody knew Rufus.

WS: What a singer, huh?

[*Warren starts singing, "For the good times…"*]

WS: Another picture from Grant Street Dancehall in Lafayette–Jimmy Vaughn, Stevie Ray Vaughan's brother. I went to see him play, then went backstage to visit.

WS: We saw him another time in Austin, when my son was with me. My son is a guitar player and Stevie Ray was his idol. My son was so thrilled to meet Jimmie Vaughan. And Jimmie Vaughan told Todd, "Well, why the heck do you want to meet me? Look, your dad is a star too!"

YL: Jimmy Vaughn knew who you were?

WS: Yes!

YL: It's crazy… ***you*** **are the star that all these guys want to meet.**

Warren Storm and Jimmy Vaughn

Warren Storm and Little Al Jackson

WS: [*blushing*] Well…I don't know about that. You see, I was a fan of theirs and they didn't know that, but they were a fan of mine, and I didn't know that either!

WS: Little Al Jackson. He's a Fats Domino impersonator. I played in Lake Charles at Yesterday's Club, and he came sing. I played drums. I told him I was a Fats Domino fan too. And we both did a Fats Domino song. He's a good little dude. That was about 1992, 1993, something like that.

Little Richard

WS: This is a picture of Little Richard. I'll tell you a secret...I never met him. Somebody just gave me a picture. [*laughing*] But, I was a big fan of Little Richard... Fats Domino, Little Richard, Jerry Lee, Chuck Willis–I learned how to sing listening to all their music.

YL: This picture caused quite a stir at UL Press. Who is this group?

WS: Sir Douglas Quintet was a band from Houston. Doug Sahm was the lead singer. And they had Augie Meyers, Jim Stallings, and Martin Fierro. We recorded for the same producer, Huey Meaux. I remember they played at a club in New Iberia. Anyway, we became good friends, me and Doug. After the Sir Douglas Quintet, Augie formed his own band, the Texas Tornados.

YL: I never heard of the Sir Douglas Quintet before.

WS: Well, that was right around the time of The Beatles and the Rolling Stones. They went to England, and people from England went crazy for them. I guess they thought they were English. But they were Texans. It was in the early 60s.

WS: Doug Sham would come listen to us when we were playing on the Thruway, six or seven nights a week. He'd just drop by at Yesterday's Club. I played there six nights a week with Tommy McLain for a couple of years.

YL: Do you think that's the highest form of flattery? When a fellow musician comes listen to your music?

WS: Oh yes. When any musician comes to hear you, it's wonderful. But when big stars come to see you, well...

WS: This was taken in Branson, Missouri, at Clay Walker's show. Grant Clement, Willie "Tee" Trahan, Clay Walker, me, and Corria Goudreaux. We were only going to hear his show, but he called me up there and I got to sing with him! I sang "Jambalaya."

Kim *Wilson, Warren Storm, Taj Mahal, and unknown*

WS: This was taken in Memphis, Tennessee. Kim Wilson, Taj Mahal, and another guy. Kim was the lead singer for The Fabulous Thunderbirds. Taj Mahal is a blues singer. They both played the harmonica too.

YL: What were you doing in Memphis?

WS: I was there for the Ponderosa Stomp. Every year they have that in New Orleans. But, when one of those hurricanes hit, they had to move it to Memphis. But them guys, they all knew who I was, man. I remember Kim introduced himself to me. He said, "Warren Storm, I'm Kim Wilson." He was famous too!

WS: That's Elvis's drummer and guitar player right there.

WS: Barbara Lynn, from Beaumont, Texas...what an artist, man. You ever heard her sing?! Lawd, Jesus, it'd blow your mind.

Top: Warren Storm and Billy Swan (Ponderosa Stomp, New Orleans, 2005)

Middle: Warren Storm, D.J. Fontana, and James Burton (Ponderosa Stomp, New Orleans).

Bottom: Barbara Lynn and Warren Storm (2003)

Warren Storm, My Brother,

I have had the pleasure of knowing Warren since I was a kid. In the '50s we played music together and occasionally still do to this day. Warren and I have traveled to many different towns playing gigs. Of course, Warren was always considered the special guest! I had the privilege to play at Gilly's in Pasadena, Texas, as the cover for Warren and Freddy Fender. He is by far the best singer and drummer I have ever played with. He is the definition of a true brother musician. To me, he is more like family, rather than simply a friend. He has a natural talent that is known all over the country. He is a self-taught musician with his own unique flair. He is definitely underestimated because he is truly one of a kind. He is not only an amazing musician, but he is also a phenomenal human being. He has helped me, as well as other musician friends of mine, get started in this tough music industry. Not once did he ever give up on us. All he had, he devoted to his music and his friends.

I'm lucky to still get together with Warren sometimes. We have traveled to places like Nashville, Pigeon Forge, Gatlinburg, and Branson. I cherish those moments playing and singing with him. He is a tireless musician. He loves reminiscing about "the old times" and recalling the fulfilling aspects of his life. I will always consider him the godfather of rhythm and blues, country, jazz, Cajun music, and of course swamp pop.

Your brother, friend, and always your biggest fan,

—Grant Clement

P.S. He is the only person I know of that Shoji Tabuchi ever called up from the audience to accompany him on stage.

Willie "Tee" Trahan, Warren Storm, Shoji Tabuchi, and daughter (Branson, MO)

[*Warren begins singing, "If you should lose me, oh yea, you'd lose a good thing…"*]

WS: Very nice lady, great singer, and she plays the guitar left handed.

WS: I saw her two years ago when we played in New Orleans for the Ponderosa Stomp.

WS: That's Shoji Tabuchi. He lived in Shreveport, Louisiana, but recorded in Crowley at J.D. Miller's in the 1970s. He had his own theatre in Branson and all the greats would go and listen to him there, but he would never call anyone up to sing with him. When we went to see him, he called me up on stage! As far as I know, I'm the only one. We sang "Jambalaya."

WS: That's Phil Phillips. He was the one that did the song "Sea of Love."

Warren Storm and Phil Phillips (New Orleans, LA)

Jimmy Elledge, Warren Storm, and Don Henley (Hall of Fame, 1995)

WS: I remember meeting Don Henley at the *Louisiana Hall of Fame* ceremony. It was held at Acadian Village. Don Henley looked at me and said, "You the star here tonight!"

Warren Storm and Boots Randolph (Ponderosa Stomp, Memphis, TN, 2006)

WS: Wow. Boots Randolph. He played sax with Owen Bradley's super star band. He recorded often with the Nashville Sound Band.

Warren Storm and Buck Trent (Branson, MO, 1999)

WS: Buck used to play electric banjo with Porter Wagoner. He came down here not too long ago to play. Nice guy.

Lazy Lester and Warren Storm (Photo by Gene Tomko)

WS: This was for a private party, which was called "Blues on the Bayou."

Warren Storm, James Johnson, Lazy Lester, Rudy Richard, Jockey Etienne, and Carol Fran
(Photo by Gene Tomko)

WS: I don't even remember where this was taken, but look at me with all those blues musicians!

WS: This is when Edwin Edwards (former governor of Louisiana), first got elected in 1972. I played for his fundraisers and stuff.

WS: Look! I didn't even have a mustache. I think I told you already, but I first started that in 1974.

Warren Storm and Edwin Edwards (1972)

Warren Storm, T.K. Hulin, and Joe Douglas

Warren Storm and Tommy McLain

Warren Storm on Passe Partout

WS: Well look at that. That's Tommy before he had his white beard. This was in the early 1970s. This was at my house, but I don't remember which one. He just came for a visit, I guess.

*Paul Marx, Warren Storm,
and C.J. Angelle (KBON Radio Station)*

Warren and I have done so many shows throughout the years on stage, in clubs, etc., and every one of them has been nothing but a blast. We traveled with Lil' Band O' Gold to many countries and Warren was always one of the crowd pleasers, to say the least.

I hope there are many more events in the future because he sure is a fun time to be with! Warren is the ultimate singer and drummer. And he is well-respected in our music family.

—TOMMY MCLAIN

Camey Doucet and Warren Storm (KROF Radio Station)

Rufus Thibodeaux and Warren Storm

WS: Rufus was a very good friend and a very good musician. Harriet would cook and he'd come eat.

WS: Lord have mercy! I just relived a big portion of my life right here.

"I played the good joints and the holes in the wall," a line from one of Warren Storm's latest releases, aptly describes the career of all of us involved in swamp pop music. Warren has been a stalwart, a devotee to a genre of music he helped to create in the late 1950s.

I first met Warren in 1958 at Fort Polk, near Leesville, Louisiana, during summer National Guard training. We developed a friendship that has endured to this day. Over all these years, I have yet to hear anyone speak negatively of him. But his personality isn't his only virtue. Warren Storm possesses a unique, distinctive voice and is an accomplished, multi-talented musician revered worldwide. One of his biggest fans just happens to be Ringo Starr!

Memories of the multitude of gigs/shows we performed together, both domestically and internationally, the fishing and hunting trips, and just the general get-togethers, has left an indelible mark in my mind and my heart. Through the long road trips, countless hours in recording studios, lengthy flights, tiresome days and nights away from home, he never lost his sense of humor. That speaks volumes. Warren Storm's life story; what a culmination to a great music career.

I love you my brother, today and forever.

P.S. Just one quick story...

On the occasion of Warren's fiftieth birthday, Joe Sonnier and I went to a cemetery and collected the oldest, driest flowers we could find. I came home and made a poster that read "Halfway between birth and dirt is where you're at right now!" That afternoon, Joe and I went to the Leu Bon Ton Lounge, the place where I was performing that night, and decorated the back of the stage with the poster and flowers.

I don't think he ever forgave me for that one!

—JOHNNIE ALLAN

Warren Storm and Johnnie Allan

Willie "Tee" Trahan, Warren Storm, and Richard LeBoeuf (La Poussiere, Breaux Bridge, LA)

Warren Storm and Marcia Ball
(Lafayette, LA, 2019)

WS: You know who that is? Marcia Ball, in Austin, Texas. She played before us I believe. Lil' Band O' Gold was playing. She's a talented, sweet lady.

I grew up listening to Warren Storm before swamp pop even had a name. It was our home-grown dance music in the honky-tonks and Catholic halls all over South Louisiana. Occasionally a song would break out, like Warren's recording of "Prisoner's Song," and the world would get a taste of what we knew and loved. There's a quality in Warren's voice that is unique to this part of the country and that Gulf Coast sound goes back to Link Davis Sr. and Bobby Charles and through Doug Sahm to Marc Broussard today. It's warm and clear, with a little catch at the end. Warren can rock out, leading the band from behind the drum set, but his repertoire of six/eight ballads is the treasure. Everyone playing Louisiana music today owes Warren thanks for his soulful influence. "My House of Memories" still gives me goose bumps down to my toes.

—MARCIA BALL

Steve Riley, Marcia Ball, Warren Storm, and C.C. Adcock
(Austin, TX)

Lil' Buck Sinegal and Warren Storm (Blue Moon Saloon, Lafayette, LA)

WS: That's me and Lil' Buck Sinegal at the Blue Moon Saloon in Lafayette, Louisiana. We've been friends forever. We played in Holland together. And, I played with him at the Ponderosa Stomp in New Orleans. I'd meet him at his house and we'd ride together.

WS: He's such a good guy, man.

Willie "Tee" Trahan, Wayne Toups, and Warren Storm

My friend Warren Storm, I had the pleasure of meeting Warren over forty-five years ago. We became friends after that and did several recording sessions together. I had the pleasure of hanging out with him at several places he played over the years.

He was always kind and respectful to me and our friendship continues today as we are in contact with each other all the time. His artistic value in the music business has helped me become a better musician and vocalist.

Warren is a true Louisiana legend and I am proud to call him my friend.

—WAYNE TOUPS

Warren Storm and Dickie Landry (Annapolis, MD, 2002)

Warren Storm and Sonny Landreth (Austin, TX)

Rufus Thibodeaux, V.J. "Boo Boo" Boulet, Bessel Duhon, and Warren Storm

YL: Out of all the pictures you gave me, this is my personal favorite.

WS: You got to be kidding! This was at some house in Lafayette. There's Rufus Thibodeaux, V.J. Boulet, Bessel Duhon, and myself. God knows what we were doing!

WS: Clarence "Frogman" Henry–that's in New Orleans at the Ponderosa Stomp. They used to have it every year but now they have it every two years.

YL: What were you doing at the Ponderosa Stomp?

WS: I was a performer. I didn't have my band. I used Lil' Buck Sinegal's band. Top notch rhythm and blues band with horns and everything. I didn't play, I just sang. Frogman was on the program as well.

WS: I had met him in the 50s. He literally sang like a frog on one of his songs, "I Ain't Got a Home." During his set, he was singing that song and I passed in front of the stage. He said (in the frog voice), "Warren Storm!"

WS: He's such a good dude, man. Down to earth just like Fats was. He used to play the piano but had to stop later.

WS: Look at the old Paw Paw's! I don't remember where this was taken. That's Johnnie Allan, Tommy McLain, me, and Rod Bernard. Rod's not doing good right now. He called me the other day. He said, "I'm calling my friends so I can remember them." He has the beginning of Alzheimer's.

Johnnie Allan, Tommy McLain, Warren Storm, and Rod Bernard

Warren Storm! That says it all. It means legend. I was just a young boy working with J.B. Perry and the Music Macks when I first heard Warren. We used to play a lot of the same clubs. Matter of fact, we usually played first at clubs like Pangay's Night Club and the Lake Shore Club, etc., and then Warren and his guys would do the late show. He was a great drummer, but he was also a great singer and entertainer. People loved him. They loved his style of music which was called "swamp pop" music. He is also considered "The Godfather of Swamp Pop" music, and rightfully so. I was lucky enough to get to do a swap pop tribute album and was able to get Warren on the project. I was so happy when I asked if he would like to do it and he said, "Yes." We had a great time in the studio and Warren was very easy to work with. He also still had the pipes he had as a young man.

I will always look at Warren as one of my heroes in South Louisiana. I hope one day that people look at me the same way that we all look at Warren Storm, the legend.

Warren, thank you for the many years of sharing your talent with *ALL* of us in South Louisiana and the world.

God bless you, man.

—SAMMY KERSHAW

WS: But you know what? I'm still older than all of them, man!

YL: Were the four of you ever in a band together?

WS: Of course, me and Rod Bernard were in a band together…for seven years with The Shondells. The four of us performed together at different venues through the years, but we were never officially in a band together.

WS: This is me and Sammy Kershaw.

YL: What was this for?

WS: Oh, we just got together to go eat lunch…just a bunch of guys going to eat lunch.

WS: A long time ago, Sammy used to bring his guitar when we played at Alex Broussard's Ranch and he'd ask, "Can I sit in?" I'd say, "Yeah, come on." And he'd sit in and sing.

WS: I met a lot of stars at the Alex Broussard Ranch. I met George Jones there a bunch of times, and Mel Tillis. I never took a picture with Mel. I wish I would have.

WS: We'd open up for them. A couple of times George Jones didn't show up, so we made a lot of money! I told his band members, "Tell him not to come next time too!"

YL: When you would open for these big stars, like George Jones, would you ever get a chance to sit and visit?

WS: Oh yes. One night, George Jones and I, we sat at the table and talked for a long time. He spent a lot of time in Lafayette. He even lived in Carencro for a few months.

"Bee Lou" Hulin, Obie Hulin, Warren Storm, Sammy Kershaw, Murray Conques, and V.J. Boulet

Hunter Hayes and Warren Storm

WS: I met Hunter Hayes at the Breaux Bridge Crawfish Festival when he was just a little boy. He's a big star now! And, he plays all the instruments.

YL: I remember Hunter's dad telling me that when he was very young, just learning to walk, he would take spoons and go by the speaker and play along with the music.

WS: They told me I did that too. I don't remember that, though. I guess I was about two or three years old.

WS: That was me and Aaron Neville. It was an award show in New Orleans. I got an award that day too! Well, the award was for Lil' Band O' Gold, The Big Easy Entertainment Award, 2001, but they gave it to me, the old man. [*laughing*]

YL: Did you ever perform with Aaron Neville?

WS: No, but I saw him perform. I met the whole family. Art, the oldest one in the family, I knew better than anyone. We did a lot of shows in the 1950s together in New Orleans. One day, I asked Art, "You think I could get a picture with Aaron?" He looked at me and said, "Well he's over there! Go ask him!" Aaron is kind of shy you know.

WS: Allen Toussaint and Warren Storm. This was for The Big Easy Award. See, I got it in my hand right there. And that, to the left is Art Neville–Aaron's brother. He's the one that knows me. He passed away man, a genius. He wrote over two or three hundred songs that were all hits and he could play the piano and everything, aw man.

WS: Art asked me one time, he said, "Warren, when are you gonna quit dying your hair?" I said, "When they run out of dye!"

Warren Storm and Aaron Neville (2001)

Art Neville, Allen Toussaint, and Warren Storm

Jo-El Sonnier, Warren Storm, and G.G. Shinn

Warren Storm, T.K. Hulin, and Tommy McLain

WS: G.G. passed away not too long ago. We took that at his club in Alexandria, Louisiana. I think it was called G.G.'s. You see, I was a guest there, every month. And Jo-El was there just to listen so we took a picture.

YL: Is his club still open?

WS: No. He shut it down. He had a club in Lake Charles, Louisiana, too, for about ten years, but I think that's closed as well.

Lil' Alfred of Cookie & The Cupcakes, Warren Storm, and Harriet Schexnider

WS: Two out of three gone in this picture. My wife and Lil' Alfred. That was for an awards night in Gonzalez, Louisiana...Lil' Alfred and Hurricane Storm. That's what we had called Harriet–Harriet Hurricane. This was in 1990. Little Alfred was a good friend and a good singer. You know, he's the only blues singer that sat at this table and ate with us. The only colored musician. That's how good a friend we were.

Ali Landry (former Miss USA) and Warren Storm

Earl Palmer and Warren Storm

Geno Delafose and Warren Storm

WS: That's Ali Landry. I met her in Simi Valley, California. Her boyfriend, well her husband now, took the picture! Can you believe I had to go all the way to California to meet her?

WS: Geno Delafose—this was the first time I met him. And you'll never guess where it was. It wasn't in Louisiana, it was in Chicago! We was on the same festival thing, man. Just like Ali Landry. I had to meet her in California. As long as you been down here in Louisiana and you hear of these people, but you never meet them. Lawd. That was at a Folk Festival in Chicago.

WS: This crazy world of music, man!

WS: Oh Lord! That's my idol drummer. The drummer of all times. He was the best drummer ever. The best rhythm and blues drummer ever. Earl Palmer, man!

WS: He played five years at Cosimo on everybody's recordings…Little Richard, Fats Domino, Shirley and Gene, and everybody. Five years he stayed at Cosimo and then he went on the West Coast, in Los Angeles. He was a session drummer. He played on the Dean Martin sessions, the Frank Sinatra sessions, everybody! And you know how he got started? He was a shoeshine boy in New Orleans, in the ghettos. I got a book on him too!

Warren Storm and Irma Thomas
(Ponderosa Stomp, September 2007)

Stanley Joseph "Buckwheat Zydeco" Dural Jr.,
Todd Schexnider, and Lil' Buck Senegal
(Ponderosa Stomp, New Orleans, LA)

Warren Storm and Herb Hardesty (Fats Domino Sax Player)
(Memphis, TN, 2006)

Charles Mann, Huey "Cookie" Thierry
(Cookie & The Cupcakes), and Warren Storm
(Podnuh's Night Club, St. Martinville, LA)

Warren Storm, Clint West, Freddie Pate, Lil' Alfred, Wayne Shuler, Tommy McLain, and Willie "Tee" Trahan (Ville Platte, LA)

Warren Storm, Hoss Childress (KBON DJ), T.K. Hulin, and Tommy McLain

Art Neville, Jon Cleary, Warren Storm, George Porter, and Herb Hardesty (New Orleans, LA)

Mike Burch, Charles Ventre, Johnnie Allen, Tony Ardoin, Warren Storm, and Steve Grisaffe (River Road Band)

Rod Bernard, Warren Storm, and Johnnie Allan (Bayou Bar, Lafayette, LA, April 1982, Photo by Paul Harris)

Warren Storm, Johnnie Allan, and Tommy McLain (Yesterdays Club, Lafayette, LA, April 1989, Photo by Paul Harris)

Johnny Adams (Festival Hall, London, England)

WS: This is the great Johnny Adams. He had a hit with "Reconsider Me." Margaret Lewis, she just passed away, wrote that song. She was from Shreveport, Louisiana. I recorded one of her songs.

[*Warren begins to sing, "We were dancing, and she held me, just like you used to…"*]

YL: You met Johnny Adams in London?

Warren Storm, Freddie Pate, and Doug Kershaw (Crowley, LA)

WS: Yes, and also, three months before he passed away, we did a benefit dance for him in Gonzales, Louisiana. When I walked in the door, he was singing "Reconsider Me." I went to the stage right away and just listened to him sing. Great singer from New Orleans. Great singer.

WS: This was at J.D. Miller's studio in Crowley, Louisiana. I think Doug was recording and we went just to listen, but Freddie and I ended up playing on the session.

WS: I been knowing Doug Kershaw since we were little. We grew up together. He's from Lake Arthur, Louisiana. We used to jam together. He's insane! [*laughing*]

WS: This was for the Ponderosa Stomp. Tony passed away just last month. Tony Joe White. He wrote two songs and he didn't have to do anything but collect royalties on those two songs. "Rainy Night in Georgia" and "Pork Salad Annie."

WS: "Rainy Night in Georgia," Brooke Benton recorded that and Elvis recorded "Pork Salad Annie." Tony was from northeast Louisiana.

WS: King Karl was the singer for Guitar Gables band. This was when my friend Chad Kassem flew us up there to do a show. Chad bought an old church in Salinas and turned it into a music space. The bandstand is where the altar was. They still had all the pews in there and everything. I played drums while he sang. It was me, King Karl, Little Bob, Carrol Fran, Lil' Buck, and all them. He flew us all out there.

WS: What a singer he was too. He sang "Irene," that's one next to Mathilda.

Tony Joe White and Warren Storm (New Orleans, 2002)

Warren Storm and Bernard "King Karl" Jolivette (Salinas, KS)

[*Warren begins to sing, "In the middle of a dream..."*]

WS: That song was recorded and came out before "Mathilda." King Karl ended up moving to Salinas where it was dryer because he had problems with emphysema down here. It was too humid.

Warren Storm and Buddy Guy (Australia, 2010)

YL: Tell me about Buddy Guy.

WS: Well, I was playing the Byron Bay Festival in Australia, and was backstage in the tent area where musicians wait to play. His tent was right next to us and I just happened to see him walking by. I asked if I could take a picture, and he was fine with that.

WS: You see, my son is a huge Buddy Guy fan. When I sent him that picture, he liked to have flipped!

One of the greatest benefits of being an entertainer is that every once in a while, you get to meet, know, and share the stage with a special, unique, and talented individual. That person to me is Warren Storm.

Not only very talented, but a great person and a great friend! Congratulations Warren! So happy that your life and career are finally put into words for everyone to cherish forever. You only get better with time. And yes! You are truly the "GODFATHER OF SWAMP POP."

—MURRAY CONQUE

Hall of Fame and Awards

YL: You're in several Hall of Fames, both in and out of Louisiana. Can you remember all of them?

WS: Well, I've been inducted into the Louisiana Music Hall of Fame. But there was two of them, and I'm in both.

YL: Why two?

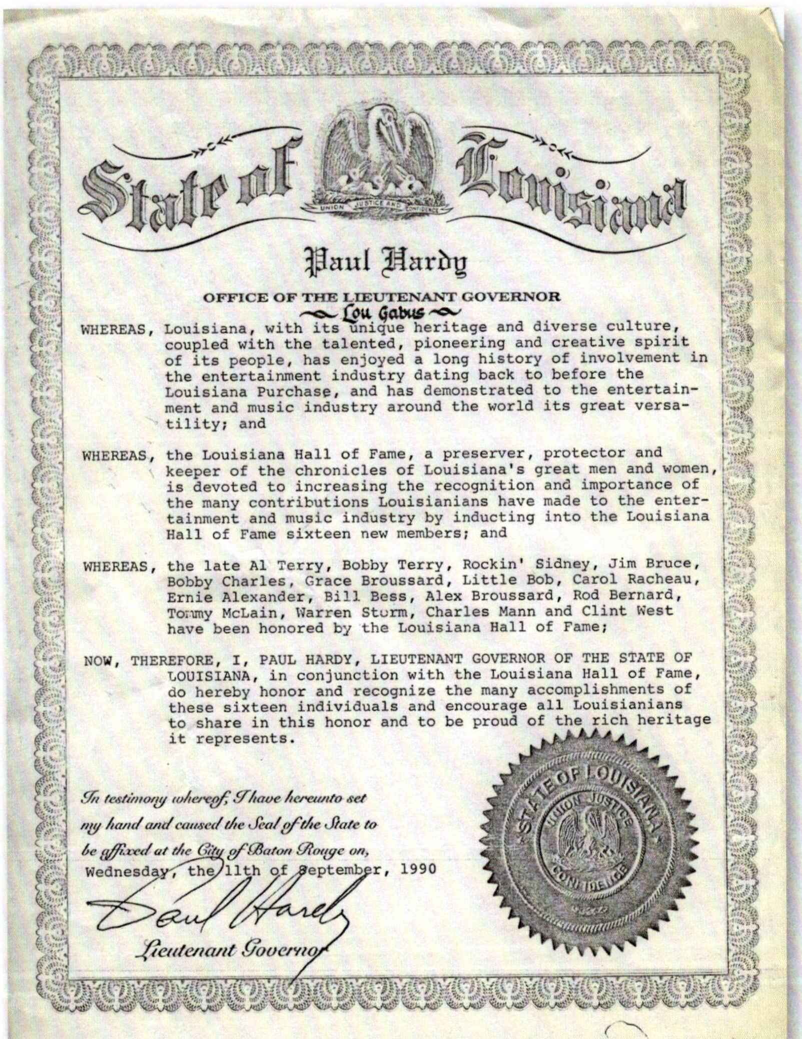
State of Louisiana

Paul Hardy

OFFICE OF THE LIEUTENANT GOVERNOR

Lou Gabus

WHEREAS, Louisiana, with its unique heritage and diverse culture, coupled with the talented, pioneering and creative spirit of its people, has enjoyed a long history of involvement in the entertainment industry dating back to before the Louisiana Purchase, and has demonstrated to the entertainment and music industry around the world its great versatility; and

WHEREAS, the Louisiana Hall of Fame, a preserver, protector and keeper of the chronicles of Louisiana's great men and women, is devoted to increasing the recognition and importance of the many contributions Louisianians have made to the entertainment and music industry by inducting into the Louisiana Hall of Fame sixteen new members; and

WHEREAS, the late Al Terry, Bobby Terry, Rockin' Sidney, Jim Bruce, Bobby Charles, Grace Broussard, Little Bob, Carol Racheau, Ernie Alexander, Bill Bess, Alex Broussard, Rod Bernard, Tommy McLain, Warren Storm, Charles Mann and Clint West have been honored by the Louisiana Hall of Fame;

NOW, THEREFORE, I, PAUL HARDY, LIEUTENANT GOVERNOR OF THE STATE OF LOUISIANA, in conjunction with the Louisiana Hall of Fame, do hereby honor and recognize the many accomplishments of these sixteen individuals and encourage all Louisianians to share in this honor and to be proud of the rich heritage it represents.

In testimony whereof, I have hereunto set my hand and caused the Seal of the State to be affixed at the City of Baton Rouge on, Wednesday, the 11th of September, 1990

Paul Hardy

Lieutenant Governor

Joe Stampley and Warren Storm (Louisiana Music Hall of Fame, Lafayette, LA)

WS: Well, Lou Gabus, she started the first Louisiana Hall of Fame in Lafayette, Louisiana. When she died, Mike Shephard created the second one in Baton Rouge, Louisiana. It's still active today.

WS: This was at the Municipal Auditorium for the first Louisiana Hall of Fame Awards. Do you know who that is right there with me? Joe Stampley. I was already inducted, but Joe was being inducted that year. I just took a picture with him.

Rockin' Sidney's wife, Rod Bernard, Lil' Bob, Vin Bruce, Charles Mann, Tommy McLain, and Warren Storm (1998)

Warren Storm and Eddy Raven
(Louisiana Hall of Fame, 1998)

Mike Shepherd and Warren Storm
(Baton Rouge, LA, 2010)

Louisiana Hall of Fame Induction (Baton Rouge, LA)

WS: This was for the first Louisiana Hall of Fame Awards, in 1998.

WS: This was the second time I got inducted into the Louisiana Music Hall of Fame. This one was in 2010.

Warren Storm with award (Photo by Gene Tomko)

REAL BLUES MAGAZINE

Fifth Annual
"Real Blues" Awards

Presented to:

Warren Storm: Take Me One More Time (Star Records)

Congratulations! You have been selected
as Winner in the Category of:

Best U.S. Swamp Pop CD Release (New)
For the Year 1998

Excellence in Musicianship — Excellence in Performance

REAL BLUES MAGAZINE

Fifth Annual
"Real Blues" Awards

Presented to:

Warren Storm

Congratulations! You have been selected
as Winner in the Category of:

Best U.S. Swamp Pop Vocalist (Male)
For the Year 1998

Excellence in Musicianship — Excellence in Performance

Real Blues Magazine *Awards (Baton Rouge, LA)*

Lifetime Achievement Award (Gonzales, LA, 1991)

B.J. Thomas and Warren Storm (Port Arthur, TX)

WS: This is Mike Shepherd. He is the one who gave me the Hall of Fame Award in 2010. That's the current Louisiana Hall of Fame.

WS: Then there was the Gulf Coast Hall of Fame that I got inducted into.

Gulf Coast Hall of Fame (Port Arthur, TX, 1999)

George Mouton, Janis Joplin look-a-like,
Harriet Schexnider, unknown, and Warren Storm
(Gulf Coast Hall of Fame, Port Author, TX, 1999)

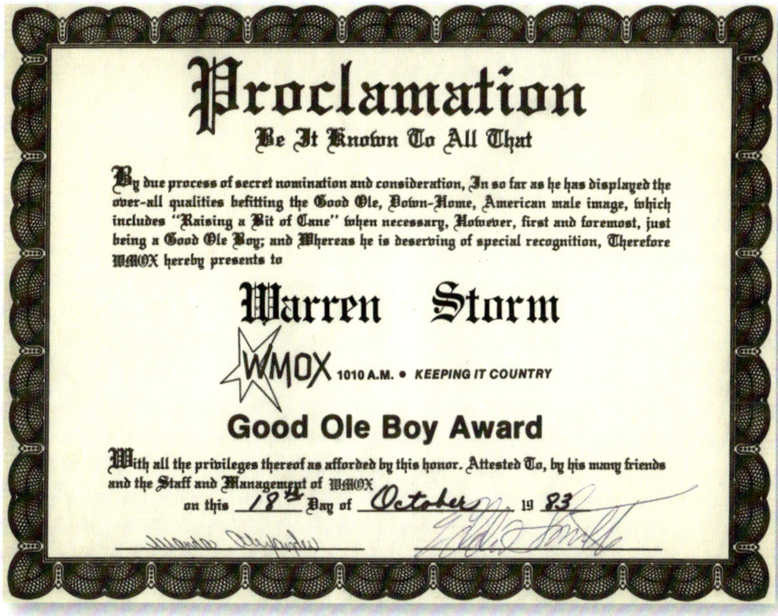

Proclamation

Be It Known To All That

By due process of secret nomination and consideration, In so far as he has displayed the over-all qualities befitting the Good Ole, Down-Home, American male image, which includes "Raising a Bit of Cane" when necessary, However, first and foremost, just being a Good Ole Boy; and Whereas he is deserving of special recognition, Therefore WMOX hereby presents to

Warren Storm

WMOX 1010 A.M. • KEEPING IT COUNTRY

Good Ole Boy Award

With all the privileges thereof as afforded by this honor. Attested To, by his many friends and the Staff and Management of WMOX on this 18th Day of October 19 83

WS: This is me and B.J. Thomas for the Gulf Coast Hall of Fame. We were both inducted in there, me, B.J., and Charles Mann. Janis Joplin's band from San Francisco was there too. That was in 1999, I believe.

YL: Why was Janis Joplin's band at the Gulf Coast Hall of Fame?

WS: They performed. They had a girl who was dressed like Janis Joplin and she sang her songs. She was good!

YL: Now this one is interesting.

WS: Yes. That was just some radio station, WMOX in Jackson, Mississippi, that gave me that. I believe that was in 1983.

YL: You're in the Louisiana Hall of Fame twice, *and* the Gulf Coast Hall of Fame, correct?

WS: Yes, and the Blues Hall of Fame in Baton Rouge, Louisiana.

WS: I got the Slim Harpo Award for the blues. I played drums with all the blues artists. The award says, "Slim Harpo Award, 2013, Warren Storm–Legend."

> Throughout the years, it's always been a pleasure and lots of fun sharing the stage with my friend Warren.
>
> Time is flying by so fast. I hope we have more fun times in store, my friend.
>
> All the best to you in the future.
>
> —Charles Mann

Promo Shots

WS: Well, look at that. That's my first promo picture I ever took.

First Promo Picture for Heart and Soul *Album (1983)*

Second Promo Picture for Heart and Soul *Album*

Warren Storm (1979)

WARREN STORM
Godfather of Swamp Pop Music
BOOKINGS
Phone 337-367-7159 / 337-789-6599
E-mail: wstorm103@aol.com
Website: www.warrenstorm.com
Photo by: Al Guidry · Portfolio 2000 337 406-0927 / 337 255-8567

Godfather of
Swamp Pop Music
WARREN STORM
BOOKINGS
Phone 337-367-7159 / 337-789-6599
Email: wstorm103@aol.com
Website: www.warrenstorm.com

Playbills and News Articles

I have known Warren almost all of my life. As a kid growing up playing in all the honkytonks, I naturally knew of Warren. Although he is a little older than me, I met him through my brother Bob Shurley, a.k.a. Red Smiley. As a young singer, Warren, even then, had a following, especially the pretty girls that followed the band. I lost track of Warren while I was at LSU Law School. Upon graduation I started playing with The Swing Kings (a group of young musicians consisting mostly of former Boogie Kings) and we played every Sunday night at the Step-Inn Club in Lawtell. On Sunday afternoons, The Shondells featuring Warren Storm, Rod Bernard, and Skip Stewart would play at the Southern Club in Opelousas and I always tried to stop and listen to the band before I had to go to my gig in Lawtell. I always enjoyed seeing Warren playing the drums and singing.

Recently I have had the opportunity to play with Warren, Willie, and Cypress. Although Warren uses a cane to get around, and sometimes sits on the bandstand as he sings, he can still sing his "a**" off. Warren just sings, no playing the drums. I especially like to hear him sing "Need Somebody Bad Tonight" and "Last Man Standing."

Warren, known wide and far as the "Godfather of Swamp Pop," is the ultimate entertainer, knows how to work a crowd, and enjoys the music as much or more than the audience. Warren is truly a legend in his own time.

—Earl Taylor
District Attorney, St. Landry Parish

YL: Tell me about Gilton's Club.

WS: That was in Eunice, Louisiana. I used to call it the "Echo Chamber." It was just a cement building, and when you'd clap your hands, it would echo forever. Can you imagine what it sounded like with a set of drums in there? The acoustics were terrible, but we played anyhow.

YL: Tell me about Philbo's Club.

WS: That was a club down there in Houma, Louisiana. I was just a guest with another band. One night only.

GRAND OPENING
Philbo Productions Presents
Recording Artist
WARREN STORM
· The Prisoners Song
· My House of Memories
· And More
ONE NIGHT ONLY - WED. OCT. 10
Philbo's
(Formerly the Round-Up)
201 Monarch Dr.
851-0815
Thurs. & Friday - Come See
The Blue Eyed Soul Revue
SPECIALS ALL WEEK AM/PM
$1.00 Slammers
$ .50 Draft

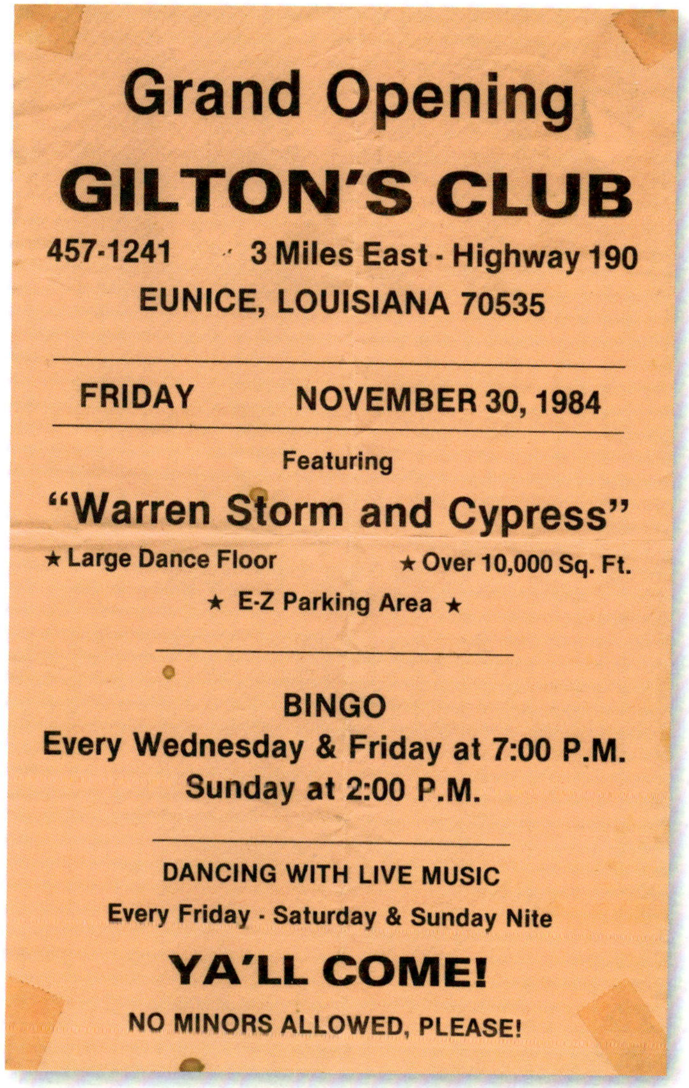
Grand Opening
GILTON'S CLUB
457-1241
3 Miles East - Highway 190
EUNICE, LOUISIANA 70535
FRIDAY
NOVEMBER 30, 1984
Featuring
"Warren Storm and Cypress"
★ Large Dance Floor
★ Over 10,000 Sq. Ft.
★ E-Z Parking Area ★
BINGO
Every Wednesday & Friday at 7:00 P.M.
Sunday at 2:00 P.M.
DANCING WITH LIVE MUSIC
Every Friday - Saturday & Sunday Nite
YA'LL COME!
NO MINORS ALLOWED, PLEASE!

Swamp Pop Revue
Swamp Pop Legends
GG Shinn TK Hulin
Tommy McLain Willie Tee Warren Storm
Johnnie Allan LA Express
April 7 in the NEW Mári Center
Paragon
CASINO • RESORT
1-800-WIN-1-WIN
LAMAR

Now Dig This, *July Issue (1995)*

WARREN STORM

THE WORKHORSE OF SWAMP POP

By SHANE K. BERNARD

Most swamp poppers are praised solely as vocalists - but Warren Storm is renowned for both his vocals and his drumming, recording several classic swamp pop songs (he remains producer J.D. Miller's top-selling swamp popper) and backing other musicians in the studio and on stage. Artists whom he has supported over the decades include fellow swamp poppers Johnnie Allan and Rod Bernard, as well as legendary blues and rhythm and blues artists like Katie Webster, Silas Hogan, Slim Harpo, Lonesome Sundown, Lightnin' Slim and Lazy Lester. Failing to re-appear on US national charts after his initial success with 'The Prisoner's Song' (Nasco 6015), Storm nevertheless remains a vital swamp pop artist in South Louisiana and East Texas, where dedicated fans continue to purchase his releases on local independent labels. Indeed, his admirers know Storm more for his many regional hits than for his isolated national hit.

He was born on February 18th 1937 in the small Cajun town of Abbeville as Warren Schexnider, a common Cajun surname of German Creole origin. He spoke only French until his third year of school and recalls impatient teachers scolding him for speaking the Cajun dialect. (His parents never learned to speak more than a few words of English.)

Storm's father, Simon Schexnider, played drums throughout South Louisiana in Cajun and country and western string bands. "He played for The Rayne-Bo Ramblers", Storm recalls, "and Happy Fats and Al Terry and Doc [Guidry]. It was a string band. It was country, then he played Cajun after that. They had two guitars, a fiddle, drums. They had an upright bass then. Most of the stuff wasn't electrified. They just had one little amplifier when they started. My daddy played music all his life. He played the guitar, the fiddle, the harmonica, the accordion and the drums." Storm recalls no other musical relatives.

Simon Schexnider taught his son to play the drums and the guitar and in 1948 Storm began sitting in with small country and western groups around Abbeville, singing tunes by artists like Faron Young, Lefty Frizzell and Hank Williams. (That same year Storm briefly met Williams at a show promoting Hadacol health tonic.) In 1952, at the age of 15, however, Storm became interested in playing music professionally after he sat in for his father at a dance. Continuing to perform Cajun and country and western music throughout high school, he joined Larry Brasso & The Rhythmaires from about 1951 to 1953. He then moved on to saxophonist Herb Landry's band, The Serenaders, around 1953 to 1956, when he played rhythm and blues for the first time. During this period Storm also performed rhythm and blues with Bobby Charles & The Cardinals. Roughly the same age, Charles and Storm often travelled together to New Orleans, where they encountered many notable rhythm and blues artists. "We'd go down there and we saw Fats Domino recording at Cosimo's studio. Then after the session we'd go to The Brass Rail - that was after-hours. And some of Fats' band performed there. Paul Gayten played piano. Lee Allen on the saxophone. And Charlie ['Hungry'] Williams - that's where I learned a lot of my drumming techniques from. Charlie Williams, that old blues drummer from New Orleans. He worked with Fats Domino and a bunch of artists. I learned [some of my drumming] from my daddy, the beginning of it. But as I'd go to New Orleans, I'd pick their style up, which is a very good style. It's like a shuffle beat with a heavy foot and a lot of cymbals."

In 1956, Storm founded his first group, a swamp pop band called The Wee-Wows. (*Wee-Wow*, explains Storm, was the exclamation of club-goers when he soloed on the drums.) At this time he exchanged the drawn-out *Schexnider* for *Storm*, a name he took from pop singer Gale Storm. The Wee-Wows soon became The Jive Masters, playing throughout central Acadiana, the Cajun region of South Louisiana. "We played everything from Cajun, country, Fats Domino rhythm and blues to Elvis Presley music", says Storm in John Broven's 'South To Louisiana', "and were booked at all the night-clubs around Lafayette, Crowley, Kaplan and Ville Platte."

Around the Spring of 1958 a Kaplan recording artist and club-owner introduced Storm to Crowley producer J.D. Miller, who invited the twenty-one year old to audition at his studio. Storm obliged, strumming a guitar as he sang

LEFT: A 1958 Nasco Records promotional photo. (Courtesy of Shane K. Bernard)

BELOW: Trade ad for Warren Storm's third Nasco release from the July 6th 1959 issue of 'Billboard'. (Courtesy of John Malcolm Anderson)

Stirring Up a Storm!
SO LONG
SO LONG
(Goodbye Goodbye)
WARREN STORM
Nasco 6028
Deejays — If you haven't received your sample copy, contact us.
NASHBORO Record Co., Inc.
Nashville, Tenn.

Now Dig This

Incorporating

ELVIS - THE MAN AND HIS MUSIC

19 South Hill Road,
Bensham,
Gateshead,
Tyne & Wear,
NE8 2XR,
ENGLAND
Tel: 0191 2624006
Fax: 0191 2342496

November 17th 1995

Dear Warren,

Please find enclosed the July issue of NDT which featured Shane K. Bernard's article on you. Hope you enjoy it!

By the way, have you heard Elvis' impromptu version of 'The Prisoner's Song'? He messed around with it (changing the lyrics somewhat!) during the 'U.S. Male' session and it has appeared on a bootleg CD. Let me know if you're interested and I'll be happy to send you a tape.

Thanks for the music,
All the best,

Trevor Cajiao

I have been knowing Warren for many years, as I am also a musician. I began playing drums and singing in 1956 at the age of fifteen with The Original Boogie Kings. It was years later that I had the pleasure of meeting Warren. And I currently produce the "Swamp Pop Legends Show" that Warren Storm in one of the guest vocalists on.

Besides his talents as a singer and drummer, I am always impressed with Warren's attitude. He is one of the most down-to-earth loving men one would ever want to meet. He is always positive and happy. I enjoy being associated with him. He is an inspiration. Thanks for this opportunity to share this.

God bless

—BERT MILLER

Terri H. Fensel/The Advertiser

Drummer and vocalist Warren Storm on the eve of the big anniversary (above), and on the Billboard charts in 1958.

GOLDEN MOMENTS

Warren Storm celebrates 50 years on the bandstand

Todd Mouton
Entertainment Editor

LAFAYETTE — He's back behind the drums. But he's not in the back seat. Swamp pop pioneer Warren Storm is the heartbeat of The Lil' Band O' Gold, an all-star amalgamation bridging the musical styles of the Gulf Coast.

Tomorrow night, the group will pay tribute to a true musical milestone — the 50th anniversary of Storm's first live gig. Equally worthy of tribute is the fact that the golden-throated entertainer has averaged five nights a week on the bandstand every week since his debut at age 11.

Throw in myriad recording sessions with legendary swamp blues artists and hits of his own, and you're looking at a truly remarkable artist.

"He's done more than any swamp pop musician to keep the live performances going," said Lafayette native Shane Bernard, author of "Swamp Pop: Cajun and Creole Rhythm and Blues" (University Press of Mississippi). "I think he is the busiest swamp pop musician out there, which is why his JIN (label) CD of a few years ago, 'Night After Night,' was aptly named."

Lafayette resident Storm went to school in Vermilion Parish with another Louisiana music icon, Bobby Charles. Both men altered their surnames to reach wider audiences (Schexnider became Storm, and Charles dropped Guidry) while forging the sound now called swamp pop. It was famously defined by saxophonist Harry Simoneaux (who played on Charles' ground-breaking "See You Later Alligator") as "half Domino and half *fais-do-do*."

'Just Because'

The Lil' Band O' Gold, which takes its name from a line in the song "Big Blue Diamonds," is dedicated to Storm and his dancehall legacy. Louisiana music, the band proclaims in tremolo guitar and accordion bursts, comes from a diverse mix of influences.

That means The Lil' Band performs vintage tunes like "Lonely, Lonely Nights" with a diatonic accordion solo, and chestnuts like "Just Because" with cascading horn and guitar lines. These older tunes, like the band's focal point, have timeless appeal.

"It's kind of ironic that it takes these young guys to bring us older guys together," bassist Dave Ranson said, referring to group organizers C.C. Adcock and Steve Riley. The pair previously formed the core of the now-defunct Cowboy Stew Blues Revue, showcasing funky jams and zydeblues guitarist Paul "Lil' Buck" Senegal on Monday nights.

The pair's Lil' Band, by the way, is anything but tiny. The group's membership includes Cajun, country, rock, blues and jazz musicians, featuring the following players and guest artists as touring schedules permit: guitarist/vocalist Adcock, accordionist/vocalist Riley, drummer/vocalist Storm, bassist Ranson, pedal steel guitarist Richard Comeaux, pianist David Egan and saxophonists Pat Breaux, Dickie Landry and David Greely.

"It's like any one person in the band could be gone," Ranson said. "But if Warren was to miss, I think that'd pretty much shut it down. What you gonna do then?"

'Prisoner's Song'

Storm had taken a 10-year hiatus from drumming, but the skills displayed on classic recordings such as Lazy Lester's "Sugar-Coated Love" and Slim Harpo's "Rainin' in My Heart" haven't dissipated.

On the latter track, recorded in J.D. Miller's famed studio in Crowley, Storm played a brush on a cardboard box in an echo chamber, creating a distinctive and highly influential snare drum effect.

When it came to his own recordings, the bilingual Storm explained, "My idol was

Domino, Chuck Willis — the soul of the rhythm and blues. ... R&B is known now as swamp pop and zydeco, but it was really the old rhythm and blues from down in New Orleans."

At 8, Storm began playing drums on his father's set, and he first performed country music three years later, sitting in one night when his dad was sick. In late June of 1958, when Storm was in his early twenties, his recording of "Prisoner's Song" on Nashville's Nasco label cracked the Billboard Hot 100. Later that year, he visited Elvis Presley at Graceland. "That was a big thrill for me. He was such a gentleman; he was just down-to-earth," Storm remembered.

Since that time, the veteran swamp popper has added a string of awards and appearances to his résumé. A regular in clubs throughout Acadiana, Storm has yet to play either the New Orleans Jazz & Heritage Festival or Festival International de Louisiane.

"We are so spoiled by the music here. There's so much music here that we just take it for granted," saxophonist Landry commented, noting that swamp pop is often overlooked.

But Storm, fellow saxophonist Breaux added, is "probably getting more powerful the older he gets." The long-running musician's secret? "If you stay straight," Storm said, playing music "prolongs longevity."

Find out what he's talking about Monday night.

- Warren Storm's Golden Anniversary Party featuring The Lil' Band O' Gold
- 10 p.m. Monday
- Swamp Water Saloon
- 1426 N. Bertrand Drive
- Admission is $4

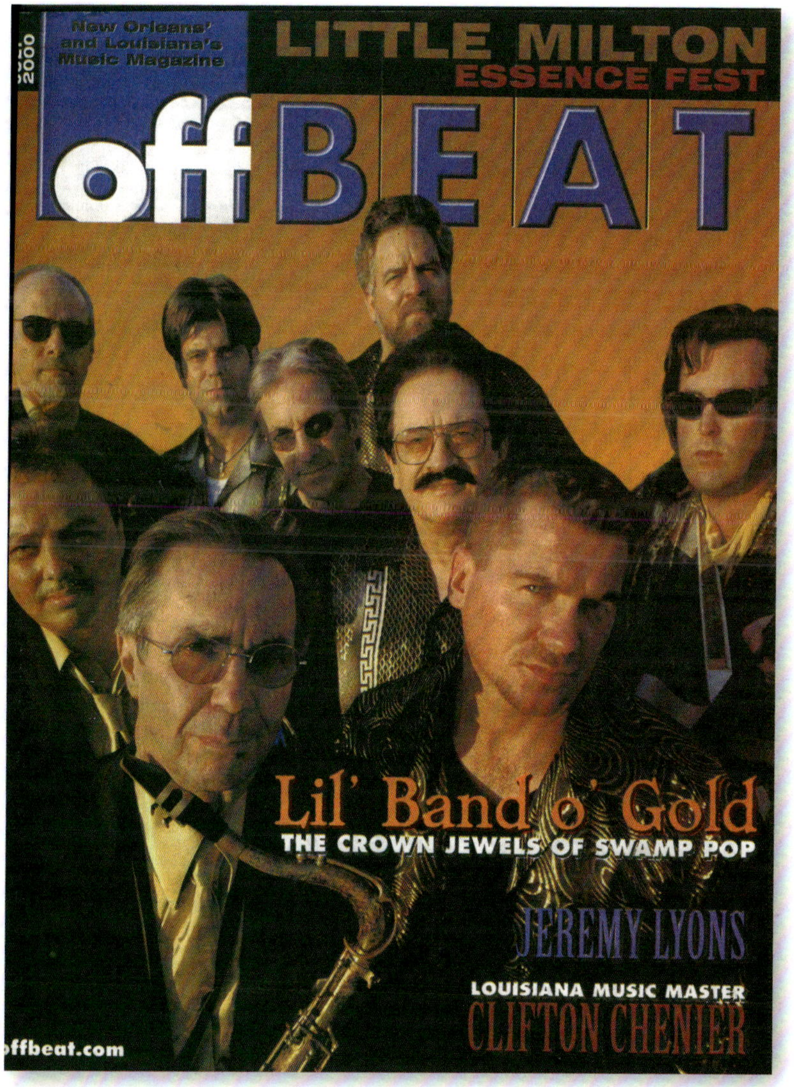

(July 2000, Courtesy of OffBeat)

Warren Storm's 80th Birthday Party

Photos by Mandie David Kiddy

YL: Tell me about your eightieth birthday party. Was it a surprise?

WS: They wanted it to be, but they had to tell me, because they were coming pick me up in a limousine!

YL: Where did it take place?

WS: In the back room at Don's Specialty Meats, in Scott, Louisiana.

WS: These are my friends who passed away, G.G. Shinn and Bernard Fontenot. Bernard was not a musician, but he was good friends with G.G. Shinn.

WS: Did you know that me and G.G. had matching walking sticks? We got them a year and a half ago. A friend from Franklin, Louisiana, made those for us.

WS: This is Benny and Linda Welch and their friend Joe. Benny, Linda, and their daughter, Alice, died in a car accident August 21, 2018. I spoke with them eight days before it happened. It was a horrific accident. We were friends for fifteen years. He was the alligator man. Gave me all kinds of alligator things. Necklaces, keychains, canes...good people, man.

WS: That's my good friend Obie Hulin. He's the one who had the party for me. He's got a print shop in Lafayette, and did all of the decorations for my party.

Left: *Warren Storm, daughters Donna and Julie, and granddaughter Heather*

WS: Can you believe I got a candle? Obie had all that made for me! Lord have mercy! I'll never forget that.

YL: Warren, this picture is pure joy!

Above: Warren Storm and Mark "Aubrey" Cole

V.J. Boulet, and Jenny and Obie Hulin

WS: This is Aubrey. He owns the place where I had my eightieth birthday party, Don's Specialty Meats.

WS: My great-granddaughter was born on the night of my birthday party. That's my great-granddaughter on the phone and my granddaughter is showing me her picture. Now she's a year-and-a-half old, Riley Ann. She lives in Ohio.

WS: Not too long ago, she was at my son's house and they called me. My son said, "Tell Paw-Paw hello." She said, "Hello Paw-Paw." I've never met her. She was born that night and I've still never seen her yet.

WS: I remember, I was singing, and I stopped, and my granddaughter came show me that picture. She was just born, February 25, 2017.

WS: Floyd Soileau, Obie Hulin, V.J. Boulet, and Bobby Badon, they all gave me an award for over sixty-eight years of playing music. It's going on seventy-one now.

WS: Earl Taylor, District Attorney of St. Landry Parish. We even had politicians there!

Warren Storm and Charlene Howard

Warren Sotem and Cammy Doucet (Local DJ and musician)

Coca-Cola

Miscellaneous Photos

WS: This was at Podnuh's Night Club in St. Martinville. I saw a lot of famous people there. I took pictures with Percy Sledge and several others there. That was a big place. Look at my leather pants! The guy on guitar is James Stelly. He's the guy that had the club. Sometimes, he played guitar with the band. He was pretty good. He doesn't play anymore though.

Mardi Gras, Podnuh's Night Club, (St. Martinville, LA, 1987)

Warren Storm (Lafayette, LA, April 1979, Photo by Paul Harris)

Warren Storm (Four Seasons, Lafayette, LA, May 1982, Photo by Paul Harris)

Warren Storm (Yesterday's Four Seasons, Lafayette, LA, April 1999, Photo by Paul Harris)

Larry Benicewicz and Warren Storm (Wolftrap Music Venue, Virginia, 2001, Photo by Carol Campbell)

WS: That's my friend Larry. Years ago, he came to Lafayette and saw my name on the marquee. I'm not sure he knew who I was, but he stopped in to listen. He started requesting songs for me to sing from the audience. When we took a break, I met him. That's when our friendship began. Since 1980, he comes down just about every year and we go all over the place listening to music. He's been a record collector all of his life. He's always finding some of my records that I don't have and sends them to me. A lot of my 45 records that I recorded on, I have because of Larry.

Ohio Musical Instrument Exposition (May 1992)

WS: This is from the Ohio Musical Instrument Exposition at the Rock-n-Roll Hall of Fame. I got a pair of my sticks in there. They got millions of drum sticks in that exhibit.

WS: Larry also writes for a blues magazine called *Blues Rag*. As a matter of fact, in this latest issue (Vol. 34, Issue 1, February 2019) Larry wrote an article about Floyd Soileau and sent it to me to read. As I was looking through the magazine, I saw that my latest CD, *Country by Storm*, had been reviewed by Dennis Rozanski. But, Dennis also reviewed *your* (Yvette Landry & The Jukes, *Louisiana Lovin'*) latest CD too! In the same magazine. How you like that?! We both in there.

Bon Amis Band (Branson, MO)

Discovering Warren Storm

—Larry Benicewicz,
Baltimore Blues Society

In many ways my discovery of Warren Storm mirrors that of Bob Hendricks. Like Mr. Hendricks, I first heard "Prisoner's Song" on the radio in the late '50s, probably at night over clear channel WLAC. And then I actually found his record at my elementary school flea market. Similarly to the art dealer, I didn't know where this mystery singer lived nor what instrument, if any, that he played. Nor was I cognizant of what particular type of music it was that he sang–swamp pop. I just took for granted that he was some C&W performer from Nashville (Nasco, his label, was based there). It wouldn't be at all an unusual presumption on my part, since Baltimore, being a factory town during World War II, had acquired a huge hillbilly population and this brand of music had quite a loyal following.

Over the years, I found more of Storm's recordings but still could not make any connection. And again, like Hendricks, I did not actually meet him until the early '80s and, finally, like Hendricks, it was purely by chance. My longtime girlfriend Carol, a photographer, had lived in New Orleans in the late '70s and she wanted to acquaint me with the sundry joys of the Crescent City. And being an R&B record collector, I didn't need a whole lot of arm twisting to agree to accompany her on her sentimental journey. But after cleaning out all the record stores in the Big Easy, I was ready for a new adventure. Not knowing who suggested it, we both decided to head northwest to Acadiana, since we both spoke a little French and were curious about the landscape and cuisine as well. Anyway, we got to Lafayette at nightfall and after securing a room at a local hotel, looked forward to going out for the evening. Not long after, I spotted a marquee on the I-49, just inside of I-10, which announced the Warren Storm show at the Checkmate Lounge. Of course, we went inside and my supposition was correct, that, since he was the vocalist (as well as drummer), he must be that long elusive entertainer who first piqued my curiosity so many years before. In any event, after the concert, which was absolutely stunning as far as musicianship was concerned, I approached Warren and introduced myself, telling him (again like Bob Hendricks) that I had been a life-long fan and was so pleased to have at last been able to see him in the flesh.

And Warren, being as he is, the host and self-appointed ambassador of goodwill for Lafayette, could not have been more affable and accommodating. To say the least, I will eternally be grateful for his paving the way for me to meet other artists of the area who sang in this swamp pop manner and whose records I also possessed, like Tommy McLain, Johnny Allan, Bobby Charles, and Rod Bernard, the latter appearing on Baltimore's Buddy Deane (teen dance) show in 1959. In short, I couldn't get enough of the music of this territory whatever form it took, and over the next two decades, I would visit the Lafayette area twice a year, whenever I got a break from teaching middle school. And it was always Warren whom I would consult first and upon whom I could count to open every door. Though he was seemingly entertaining every night, he'd at any opportunity make time for me to go out and see a zydeco show or a Cajun group, like Octa Clark or the Touchet Brothers, both on one memorable Sunday afternoon. Having performed with every outfit of every musical persuasion in this bayou country since his formative years, he knew all the performers and they, in turn, held him in very high esteem. Moreover, as far as I was concerned, they trusted his judgment even if they would normally be hesitant to roll out the welcome mat to me, a "Yankee" invader.

In fact, it would not be an exaggeration to say that this fortuitous contact with Warren Storm profoundly affected my life, since, undoubtedly, it was his encouragement that was a major factor in my becoming a blues journalist. And, believe me, due to Warren's intercession, there were many strange and wonderful stories waiting to be revealed there in South Louisiana, the grist of many of my future articles for a variety of magazines both here and abroad. Furthermore, as a result of these interviews, I, too, developed a relationship with many of these artists so that I eventually became an agent for zydeco and Cajun acts, bringing them to the Mid-Atlantic region. Indeed, how different my existence would have been without this accidental encounter one sultry July night in 1982. In all honesty, whatever I have made of myself, I owe much to Warren Storm.

Warren Storm (Lake Charles, LA)

Ponderosa Stomp
(New Orleans, LA, Photo by Gene Tomko)

Warren Storm (London, England)

Derek Huston, Beau Thomas, Chris French, Warren Storm,
Sonny Landreth, Eric Adcock, Gary Usie, Roddie Romero,
(front) Yvette Landry, and Steve Nails

THE MAKING OF

TAKING THE WORLD, BY STORM

A REGIONAL ROOTS JOURNEY WITH THE GODFATHER OF SWAMP POP

DOCKSIDE STUDIO
MARCH 2019

WHILE INTERVIEWING WARREN, the idea arose of re-releasing some of his old recordings to accompany the publication of this book. But I soon asked myself, "Why not just record a new album with Warrren? He's 82, but he still sounds incredible." So we went ahead and made an album, an album like the ones Warren had recorded many times in his career—straight to two-track tape, no digital overdubs, all in the room like in the good old days, LIVE.

We started with a core band, Eric Adcock (piano), Chris French (bass), Roddie Romero (guitar), Derek Huston (sax), and Gary Usie (drums). But once word got out about what we were up to, the project grew quickly. Marc Broussard, one of Warren's biggest fans, joined the effort, as did Beau Thomas (fiddle), Richard Comeaux (steel guitar), Willie "Tee" Trahan (saxaphone), Sonny Landreth (slide guitar), and I even jumped in on a song. Before we were done, we even wound up with a lagniappe guest performance by Creedence Clearwater Revival's John Fogerty, who Warren had recorded with back in the 1980s.

The resulting recording has everything you've been reading about in this book—more great work from one of Louisiana's iconic musicians, a consummate performer in the studio, and a man who commands the respect and love of the many professional musicians who have had the opportunity to know and work with him.

YL: Tell me, Warren, what was it like going into the studio at eighty-two years old and recording like you did when you were twenty-one?

WS: It's even more amazing than ever before.

YL: How so?

WS: Well, it's something to see all those young musicians playing the music we played fifty-something years ago. It's old music, but somehow, they make it fresh and new.

Dockside Recording Session (Photos by Gene Tomko)

Dockside Studio (Photo by Gene Tomko)

Justin Tocket, recording engineer (Photo by Gene Tomko)

V.J. Boulet and Warren Storm (Photo by Gene Tomko)

Left and above: Warren Storm and Yvette Landry
(Photos by Gene Tomko)

Yvette Landry and Warren Storm (Photo by Daniel Sanda)

EW ORLE

Warren Storm and Sonny Landreth
(Photo by Gene Tomko)

Willie Tee and Warren Storm (Photo by Gene Tomko)

Warren Storm (Photo by Gene Tomko)

Chris French, Erick Adcock, Willie "Tee" Trahan, Warren Storm, Yvette Landry, Gary Usie, Roddie Romero, and Derek Huston (Photo by Gene Tomko)

Yvette Landry, V.J. Boulet, Warren Storm,
Sonny Landreth, and Chad Kassem (Photo by Gene Tomko)

Richard Comeaux and Warren Storm
(Photo by Gene Tomko)

Marc Broussard
(Photo by Yvette Landry)

Let's wrap it up...

YL: In a conversation I had with our friend Herman Fuselier, the question came up as to the future of swamp pop. He specifically asked, "How does swamp pop survive after you, T.K. Hulin, Tommy McLain, Johnnie Allan, Rod Bernard, and the others are gone?"

WS: Hopefully, there will be some young people listening now that will be able to carry on the tradition. It takes the younger generation to keep it alive.

YL: I don't know many young people listening to swamp pop. Do you really think it'll survive?

WS: Oh...I don't know...but I know they do have people closer to the New Orleans area that are listening to that style of music. Hopefully, the children coming up listening to their parents play will continue playing it. I'm hopeful though. Good music never dies.

WS: You know, I tell everybody I see, and I tell all the musicians, Yvette's writing a story about my musical life. About my life history, about my music.

WS: I can't find the words to describe how I feel. I'm excited, happy, that God let me live this long to have this done. And I'm going to say that whenever we have the book release!

WS: You know this really is an awesome miracle. I only met you [Yvette], there's a year. That right there in itself is awesome. Thank you, Jesus, Lord have mercy.

YL: Do you think you'll ever retire?

WS: [*laughing*] No, man, musicians don't retire, and they don't die either. They just play away.

YL: Do you think that you would have had the same musical experiences if you were born in another state?

WS: Absolutely not. What we have here, in Louisiana, our area especially, is so unique. You can't find that anywhere else. People come here to visit and never leave, and it's because of the music, food, and people. It's our culture. It's special here, man.

YL: If you had to do it all over again, would you do anything different?

WS: Nope. I'd do it all the same. I love how it went from the beginning and can't wait to see what the future brings with this book and my new record. Life at eighty-two years young is pretty exciting!

YL: One last question, how does Warren Storm want to be remembered?

WS: Well...I guess I want people to remember me as someone who just enjoyed life and playing music. I always knew that I was born to do that. It's what I've done all my life. It's what I'll do until I can't do it no more.

"It makes me happy to see people smile and dance when I perform. I love that almost as much as I love making music."

Ponderosa Stomp (New Orleans, LA, Photo by Gene Tomko)